THE LAST WORD ON *THE HOWLING* SAGA THAT REDEFINED HORROR...

FROM JOE DANTE TO JOE NIMZIKI

Text copyright © Miami Fox Publishing 2018

The Howling © 1981 Embassy Pictures. All rights reserved.
Howling II: Your Sister is a Werewolf © 1985 Hemdale., Philippe Mora. All rights reserved.
Howling III: The Marsupials © 1987 Bancannia Holdings Pty. Ltd., Philippe Mora. All rights reserved.
Howling IV: The Original Nightmare © 1988 Allied Entertainments Group PLC. All rights reserved.
Howling V: The Rebirth © 1989 Allied Vision. All rights reserved.
Howling VI: The Freaks © 1991 Allied Entertainments Group PLC. All rights reserved.
Howling VII: New Moon Rising © 1995 Allied Entertainments Group PLC. All rights reserved.
The Howling: Reborn © 2011 Anchor Bay Films. All rights reserved.

Howling IV: The Original Nightmare © 2018 www.forschedesign.com. All rights reserved.
lifemasks@forschedesign.com

Every effort has been made to source and contact copyright holders.
If any omissions do occur, the publisher will be happy to give full credit
in subsequent reprints and editions.

Editor: Paul Knappett
Design: Miami Fox Publishing

The publisher would like to give special thanks to all who generously
contributed interviews and images for inclusion in this book.

Published by Miami Fox Publishing
First edition May 2018
ISBN: 978-1-9995848-0-1
www.miamifoxpublishing.co.uk

Did you enjoy reading this book? We love to hear from our readers.
Please email us at: info@miamifoxpublishing.co.uk

No part of this publication may be reproduced, stored in a retrieval system, or transmitted,
in any form or by any means without the prior written permission of the publisher, nor be
otherwise circulated in any form of binding or cover other than that in which it is published
and without a similar condition being imposed on the subsequent purchaser.

Printed and bound in UK

Contents

Foreword 6

Introduction 9

Gary Brandner 10

The Howling: First Blood 16

The Howling 22

Howling II: Your Sister Is a Werewolf 38

Howling III: The Marsupials 50

Bill Forsche 62

Howling IV: The Original Nightmare 70

Howling V: The Rebirth 90

Howling VI: The Freaks 100

Howling VII: New Moon Rising 112

The Howling: Reborn 118

Image Credits 136

Foreword by Philippe Mora

The late producer John Daly looked at me in his Sunset Boulevard office and said: "There is good news and bad news. The good news is you are going to make *The Howling II*, the bad news is that you have to make it behind the Iron Curtain in Prague. The crew will be Czech and you will have interpreters. OK, onwards and sideways."

It was 1984, and shortly after in Prague I found myself talking to a Russian officer. "What is a werewolf?" he asked. I replied: "A werewolf is a man or woman who turns into a wolf when there is a full moon." This man looked like he could kill a pig himself and eat it raw. He stared at me. Suddenly, to my huge relief, he burst out laughing and said via the translator: "You have less than an hour to finish filming your scene. Then the werewolves have to leave three at a time every ten minutes. A group like this is illegal." With that I finished a riotous scene of real Czech punks going crazy, watched by my werewolf hunter, Christopher Lee.

I had made the horror film *The Beast Within* for United Artists when I was offered *The Howling II*. As a director one is damned if you do and damned if you don't regarding sequels. If you make it, the fans of the original become rather hysterical if you do not slavishly copy the original. If you do copy the original, one is lambasted by others for lack of originality or worse. I opted to ignore the original, and so initiated the longest series in film history of sequels that have basically nothing to do with each other.

I needed a job and I was fascinated by the idea of making a film behind the Iron Curtain. The Cold War was in full swing. I was encouraged by remembering my friend screenwriter Arthur Ross saying he wrote *The Creature From the Black Lagoon* because he needed a station wagon. Christopher Lee was also a plus because we had worked together in *The Return of Captain Invincible* and he had done some brilliant musical numbers. The producer John Daly had encouraged me to make *The Howling II* outrageous, but sadly even he balked when I suggested singing werewolves.

In Greek mythology Zeus transformed Lycaon into a wolf in retaliation for Lycaon serving him human flesh. In a move that would delight Hollywood special effect houses, Zeus then killed Lycaon's fifty sons with lightning bolts. Thus horror is central to the werewolf's "origin" story.

Lycanthropes permeate European folkloric history with even Cranach the Elder making a wood cut of a werewolf attack in 1512. Researching the cinematic origins of these afflicted creatures I discovered the fascinating career of Curt Siodmak (1902-2000). His movie breakthrough was writing the iconic *The Wolf Man* (1941), starring Lon Chaney, Jr. From scratch he created several werewolf myths including the monster's vulnerability to silver bullets and the poem:

Even a man who is pure in heart,
And says his prayers by night
May become a Wolf when the Wolfbane blooms
And the autumn Moon is bright

But most fascinating was that, as a Jewish writer, he had escaped Nazi Germany, and later said the Werewolf for him was a metaphor for Jews being persecuted. The Werewolf was an innocent being chased by rabid mobs. This twist in the

Wolfman's movie provenance explains Lon Chaney's suffering and anguish when he turns into a "monster". We sympathize with him and I believe this sympathy is central to the film's eternal success. Chaney's wrenching performance pulled this character into a higher theatrical league.

I would surmise that Siodmak had also read Sigmund Freud's pioneering psychological work, *The Wolf Man*, about a patient, Sergei Pankejeff, published in 1918. Daniel Goleman, in the New York Times, wrote the following:

"Freud's key intervention with the Wolf Man rested on a nightmare in which he (the Wolf Man) was lying in bed and saw some white wolves sitting on a tree in front of the open window. Freud deduced that the dream symbolized a trauma: that the Wolf Man, as a toddler, had witnessed his parents having intercourse. Freud, amusingly theorizing that the Wolf Man had seen his parents have sex 'doggy style', thus initiated a strong sexual aspect to the werewolf myth."

Hollywood, bashful but prurient, embraced that aspect and it permeates all the *Howling* sequels, werewolf style.

This book, despite the grisly, grand guignol past of our snarling heroes, is a really fun and energizing read. But it's not superficial fun. It chronicles a cultural phenomenon: the enduring success of the only non-related film series in movie history, linked only by anguished humans turning into wolf-like creatures and howling at the moon. Lycaon had hairy legs in more ways than one. ∎

- PHILIPPE MORA

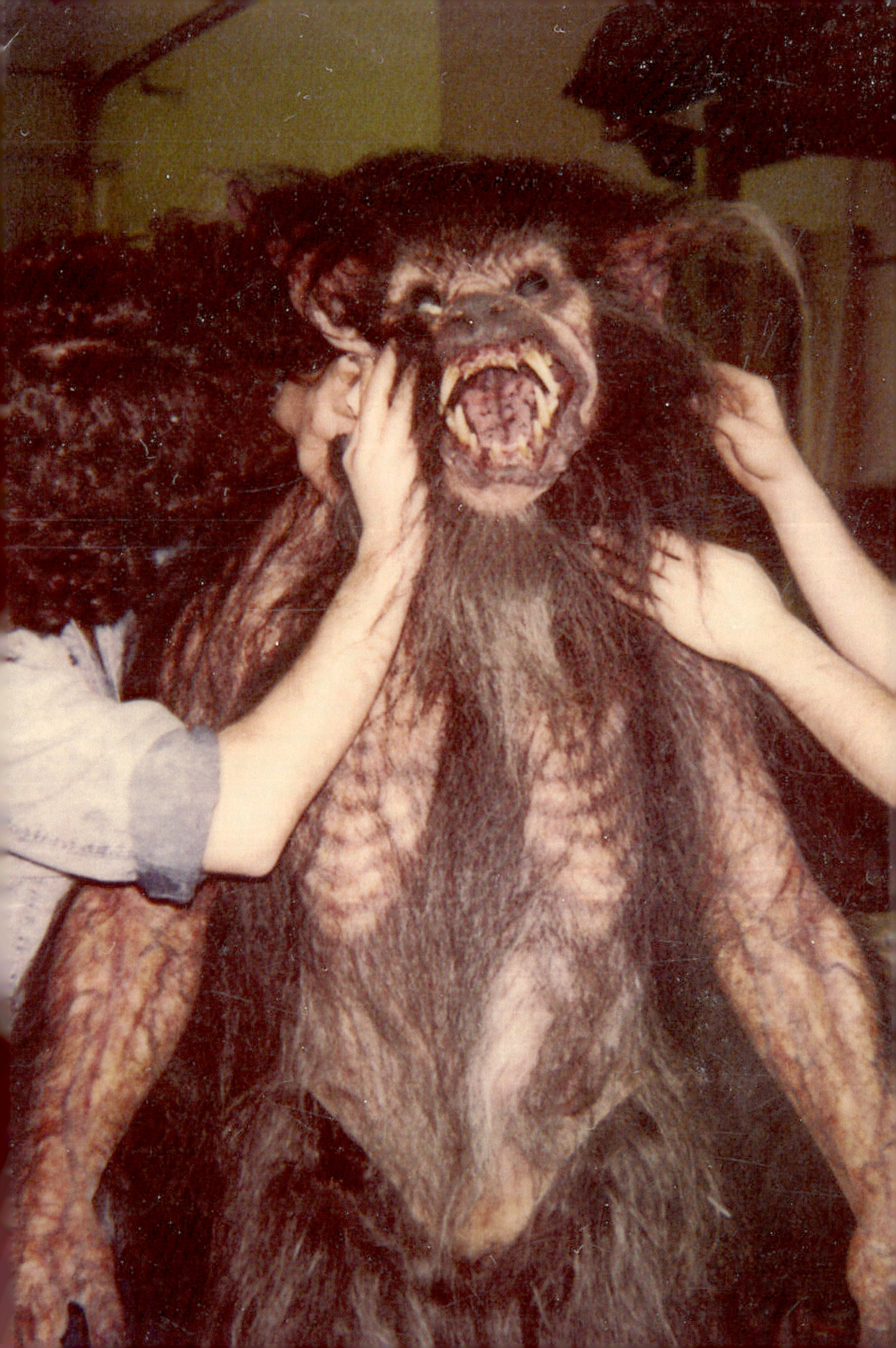

Introduction

I'm not going to lie when I say *The Howling* franchise is not high end art and not all the films within the series can even be deemed high concept movies, yet I still find *The Howling* series endearing in its variable quality.

During the writing of this book and throughout any press interviews I have done when promoting its release I have been asked many times, "Why *The Howling*?" and I've always chalked off my answer with a witty throwaway comment, "Cash!"

But a more truthful answer is that the franchise is my guilty pleasure. I have a quirky taste in horror films that hasn't always done me any favours when trying to pass myself off as a serious horror connoisseur, particularly when walking among old timers such as Allan Bryce (*The Dark Side*) and Kim Newman (*Empire*).

Many years ago *Empire* (if I can recall correctly) ran a Halloween Top Ten and invited me to the party to provide my favourite horror films. My list included *Howling IV: The Original Nightmare*, *Night of The Demons*, *Pet Sematary II* and other head-scratching inclusions. It drove online horror forums and blog spots crazy! I was called a 'moron,' a 'shambolic mess,' and 'a grade A prize prick'. Such comments left me with distain for the horror community and I genuinely felt there was something wrong with my taste in films. How can so many people be so right and me so wrong?!

Yet as time went by and maturity kicked in, on reflection those brutal comments were nothing more than forced opinion because I didn't follow the herd. Why does *The Howling* (1981) need to be my number 1 werewolf movie? Why do I have to have a Wes Craven film as part of my staple horror diet, and why can't I prefer *Friday the 13th Part III* (1982) over its original source material?

Part of my inspiration for writing this book was my love of the fourth *Howling* movie. Sure, the dubbing is awful, the performances are bad and we only get 5 minutes of werewolf action but the movie gave me a sugar rush that Joe Dante's outing didn't achieve and *Howling IV* was in fact the first werewolf movie besides *The Curse of the Werewolf* (1961) I had ever consumed.

What I'm trying to say is, whether you're taking *The Complete History of The Howling* home for *Howling II* or *The Howling: Reborn*, it doesn't matter what other people's opinions are as long as you enjoyed the movie. To damn with forced favourites and must-include films to make you an accepted member of the In Crowd; it's you that is viewing the film and if it rocks your boat be loud and proud.

Here's to *The Howling* and *Howling IV: The Original Nightmare*. Yup, there I said it, *Howling IV*!

Bryn Curt James Hammond
England, April, 2018

GARY BRANDNER

GO BEHIND THE VEIL OF THE AUTHOR THAT REDEFINED HORROR

"If you haven't read Gary Brandner you're missing a treat."
STEPHEN KING -

Gary Brandner's name may only ring a distant bell to most horror fans but the underappreciated master of horror has created some of the genre's most interesting stories, including *The Howling*.

Born on May 31, 1930, in the city of Sault Ste. Marie, a relatively isolated community in northeast Michigan that began life as a fur-trading settlement, Gary spent most of his childhood deep in the forest's undergrowth and around the sun-draped waters near to his home, where his father Phil Brandner was a forest ranger. Gary's mother, Beda Gehrman Brandner, was a traditional housewife, who stayed home to care for Gary's younger brother, Crosby, and would prepare warm meals for when the men of the family returned home after a long day maintaining the forest's campground facilities and trails and helping with the prevention of forest fires.

During his formative years the young Brandner had set his sights on becoming a writer, and his mind would often drift off into his own world of make-believe, much to his father's annoyance. But it was that very same imagination, which would frequently drift around the whirlpool of the macabre, particularly Frankenstein, Dracula and Werewolves, that brought praise from his teachers and made him the most talented scholar of his class. His teachers were so impressed by the quickly maturing writer that they would have him showcase his stories to the class, and his English teacher was the driving force that encouraged Gary to take up writing as a career.

His father wasn't fond of Gary's dreams of moving to the big city to become a writer, and although supportive of his son's ambitions, he still insisted on Gary continuing in his footsteps as a forest ranger; after all, it paid the bills and put food on the table. But Gary had bigger fish to fry and stuck firmly to his ambition of becoming a printed author. Assisted by the guiding hand of his English teacher Gary decided to test the water before diving straight into the deep end, and with an active interest in sport he came to the conclusion that he would fulfil his goal of being a writer by becoming a sports journalist.

By 1955 Brandner was a fully-fledged journalism graduate of the University of Washington in Seattle. Following his graduation he stumbled into the job of writing scripts for live TV, and to make ends meet he would pen material for stand-up comics who performed in nightclub lounges and smoky bars in and around Portland, Oregon.

Disillusioned by the way his career was panning out, Brandner decided to try settling down, and he married Paula Moon. Their marriage, however, was short-lived, and the couple soon divorced. Gary moved to California to learn to play the guitar so he could complete his quasi-beatnik persona. While taking guitar lessons the budding author was employed as a technical writer of manuals for the aerospace industry. He began writing stories, which he submitted to

various news outlets, his genre of choice – fiction! Brandner sold his first story, *A Lesson in Larceny*, to *Ellery Queen's Mystery Magazine* in 1969. *EQMM* was a popular monthly digest-sized magazine that specialised in crime fiction, particularly detective fiction.

With *Ellery Queen's Mystery Magazine* under his belt, Brandner took the next step in his career and began contributing to other periodicals, such as *Alfred Hitchcock's Mystery Magazine*. He crafted several recurring detectives that were a hit with readers due to their hard-boiled-soft-boiled, thrill-seeking personas, eager to dig into the deepest and darkest corners of society to uncover lies, deadly deception and murder most brutal.

With his career going in the right direction Brandner, who had become an avid jazz fan, decided to roll the dice for a second time on the marriage roulette table and got hitched to Barbara Nutting. Once again his career, with the uncertainty of where his next pay cheque was coming from and whether or not he could put food on the table, put a strain on the marriage, But Brandner refused to give up his lifelong ambition and kept going down the road, which was lonely at times, even with the knowledge of its pitfalls and heartbreaks. He would later recount these very real struggles to the reference guide, *Contemporary Authors*: "Kiss security goodbye, no more paid vacations, sick leave, health insurance, Christmas bonuses." But he also told them of the rewards: "In return you get to create your own fictional world, reward the good guys, and punish the bad as doesn't always happen in real life."

With several short stories complete, and a handful of quick and engaging novels under his belt that included *The Big Brain*, *The Beelzebub Business* and *Energy Zero*, Brandner ventured into the whirlpool of the macabre, which had so often engaged him as a child, and with that *The Howling* was conceived. It was published in 1977 and quickly established the author as a horror writer. Readers were titillated by the pulp horror gusto and relished the colourful energy of graphic sex, biting violence and an overall clinging atmosphere of Brandner's oppressive focal point. His agent, however, was not at all enthusiastic about Brandner's chosen subject matter, stressing that it would not sell the volumes needed to even pay the printing bill, and even if Brandner broke even he could damage his credibility as a writer.

The Howling left Brandner's literary agent shell-shocked as the novel became a runaway success and received critical acclaim. Readers wanted more, and Gary gave them more, writing *Return of The Howling* (*The Howling II*), which was published in 1979 and picks up three years after the events of the first book.

Brandner's adrenaline-pumping first novel soon caught the eye of Hollywood and he was approached to sell the rights to *The*

> **Brandner took the next step in his career and began contributing to other periodicals, such as *Alfred Hitchcock's Mystery Magazine*. He crafted several recurring detectives that were a hit with readers due to their hard-boiled-soft-boiled, thrill-seeking personas, eager to dig into the deepest and darkest corners of society to uncover lies, deadly deception and murder most brutal.**

Howling for an exorbitant sum. The author agreed, and Embassy Pictures, International Film Investors and Wescom Productions began the process of adapting Brandner's novel for the screen. After several drafts by Jack Conrad (the original director, who left following difficulties with the studio) and Terence H. Winkless proved unsatisfactory, director Joe Dante was hired and brought on board John Sayles to completely rewrite the script.

A short time later Brandner found himself at the screening of his own book. As the final credits rolled Brandner was left with his head in his hands. He hated the film and was displeased by the studio's tampering with his source material. He disassociated himself from the movie and continued writing books.

In 1984 Brandner was invited to become involved in the writing of *Howling II*, but several drafts later he removed himself from the project.

Howling III: Echoes was published in the same year that *Howling II: Your Sister Is a Werewolf* hit cinemas and it was noted for its discontinuities from his previous two books. Gone were the eerie howling noises in the dead of night and the horrific discovery that nowhere is safe. The mile-a-minute breathtaking suspense of the first two novels had been adapted to suit the new generation of book reader, and fans of the first two books were dissatisfied with Brandner's standalone plot and heavily re-imagined mythology. While fans didn't enjoy the third outing as much as the previous books *Howling III: Echoes* still saw a healthy return.

By the mid-eighties Brandner's novels had become a staple diet for horror fans, and a number of his books and short stories followed the same pattern as *The Howling*. *Walkers* was adapted for television as *From The Dead Of Night*, starring Lindsay Wagner, Bruce Boxleitner and Diahann Carroll. Once again, the original novel was changed extensively for the TV dinner consumer audience. Brandner later penned a number of feature film scripts and wrote the monetization of the feature film *Cat People*, which was released theatrically on April 2, 1982 and grossed approximately $7 million at the box office. *Cat People* received mixed reviews upon its initial release, and has since gone on to be considered an overlooked gem.

While Brandner continued to go back and forth between film and book he churned out several sleeper hits, which included the novels *The Brain Eaters*, *The Wet Good-Bye* and *Carrion* before writing both the novel and the screenplay for *Cameron's Closet*. The film was given a limited theatrical release by SVS Films in January 1989 and received mixed reviews from both critics and ticket buyers.

During his 50 years residency in southern California Gary wrote every day without missing a heartbeat, and throughout the end of the eighties and late nineties he wrote *Floater*, *Doomstalker* and *The Boiling Pool*, to name but a few.

Following his second divorce Brandner married his wife of 25 years, Martine Wood. After fulfilling his lifelong ambition of becoming a successful author he began to wind down. He became a member of several literary and film panels and taught writing classes. Because he thought a writer's life dull, Brandner often embellished accounts of his own life, so it is hard to say what was fact and what indeed was fiction, but I'm sure his claims of having to fight off sharks in a coral reef and put out oil fires in Saudi Arabia were untrue.

Gary died of oesophageal cancer on September 22, 2013. His friends still reminisce about the legendary parties he and his wife threw in his later life, right up until the 1994 Northridge earthquake, when many people moved out of state. Others remember how honest, kind and upfront he was, and that he didn't bow down to anyone, no matter who they were.

Douglas D. Hawk, in his blog *Dweller*

by the Dark Stream, wrote of his memory of Gary Brandner, "Gary and I met at an evening social/cocktail party. He was warm and amiable and we chatted about the meeting and writing. A Famous Writer was also in attendance. The FW brought a videotape of the *Eerie, Indiana* TV pilot. He set it up at a table in the corner and announced that he would be playing it for anyone interested. A couple of people joined him while the rest of us remained in the central part of the room, drinking quantities of alcohol and talking.

"Suddenly, Famous Writer yelled angrily, 'Hey, you people want to hold it down? We're trying to watch this pilot. I went to a lot of trouble to get it.'

"Gary was clearly annoyed at the FW's attitude in so far as the rest of us, probably 40 or 50 people, were being scolded by the FW and his two sycophants.

"'F— off, (FW),)' he yelled in response.

"Hey, you people want to hold it down? We're trying to watch this pilot. I went to a lot of trouble to get it!"

"There was a tense moment and, quite shocked, I thought FW might march over and go to blows with Gary. Didn't happen. FW and his followers returned to their video and the rest of us returned to our conversations and drinks.

"Gary glanced at me. '(FW) is such an asshole.'

"I really admired Gary Brandner for not kowtowing to the FW and, believe me, many other attendees did."

Yvonne Montgomery, the award-winning author of *Edge of the Shadow*, also recalled her brief encounter with Gary: "I met him once at a conference, and he was an engaging guy. Sorry to hear of his death. No more unauthorized dying!"

Gary Lake, another blogger, said of Brandner's passing, "I met him once at a convention. I wasn't a fan of his book *The Howling*, I found it drab, but after meeting Gary I realized that he had real passion and was not the ass I thought he was for slating icon Joe Dante. I revisited the books and totally looked at them in a different light. I admire the guy. It's a sad day for Horror!"

Gary Brandner was a talented writer in more ways than one, and he spread his writing ability right across the board. His work will forever live on in print and celluloid, and whether or not you are a fan, one thing will always stand out – he was a dedicated writer and husband, and he will be sadly missed. R.I.P.

"The first one that really counted was *The Howling*. My agent read my outline and told me it would never sell. A month later Fawcett bought it. It was made into a pretty good horror flick, spawned a couple of sequels, gave me a recognizable credit, and provides a virtual annuity. No wonder I love wolves." - Gary Brandner ■

THE HOWLING
FIRST BLOOD

Story by **NICK STEAD**

Mournful are their cries to the ears of men, mournful and haunting. To Mike's tormented mind they were calling for their lost sister, calling her back from the darkness she now resided in. The night rang with their pleas for her to return to them, the woods echoing with their sorrow. And yet there was something about the sound that filled him with dread, like a sinister undertone to the sombre chorus, an evil lurking beneath the seemingly innocent surface.

Nature's phantom came slinking through the trees, a dense mist coiling round the trunks and wreathing the land in its ethereal blanket, working with the shadows to limit any visibility the moonlight might otherwise have afforded. But Mike didn't need to see what was lurking in the blackness. He knew all too well what was making those cries, and he was under no illusion as to what he was to them. A rustling in the undergrowth was all it took to wear away the last of his nerves, his heart pounding as much with fear as the physical exertion of fleeing the unseen terror.

His hunters made little noise as they gave chase, and yet the young man knew with a terrible certainty that they were closing in. He caught a glimpse of something to his right, no more than a dark shape in the murk, briefly illuminated by a strong beam of ghostly light from the pale orb overhead. It was enough to drive him to greater speeds, pushing his body to its limits. And then she appeared in front of him from out of nowhere and the next thing he knew he was stood gaping at her while his chest heaved, lungs struggling to repay the debt of oxygen his muscles had built up.

Her very presence was impossible,

somehow risen from the grave whole and every bit as beautiful as she had always appeared on the news. Karen White, a woman he had often fantasised about in life and who now haunted him in death. A single tear ran down her cheek as she looked at him with those startling blue eyes, the unnatural glow full of such sadness that he couldn't help but feel sorry for the monster she was about to become. Mike knew he should keep running before the rest of them came in for the kill, yet morbid fascination would not let him turn away from the change she was going through.

And while he stood there, helpless in the hold this woman had over him, he felt something clamp down on his leg, tugging sharply so that he crashed to the ground. There he found himself face to face with a sight that filled him with a far greater horror than Karen's transformation. His brain had only one response to that horror – he screamed.

Mike was still screaming when he awoke to the unpleasant sensation of cold sweat coating his skin with its icy sheen, his bedding drenched with it. The sheets pulled at his flesh as he sat upright, as if the nightmare had been so powerful it had possessed his bed, giving it a reluctance to release him from the clutches of his night terrors. It had been the same for the past week, ever since he'd witnessed Karen White's final broadcast before her untimely death. Yet facing the nightmare wasn't getting any easier, the fear it induced in him lingering on even as he sought to calm his thundering heart and rapid breathing. And though he was firmly back in reality for what remained of the night, still the howling rang in his ears, sounding loud and clear from somewhere just outside.

The sun felt far too bright the next morning, Mike's head pounding its complaint at the lack of sleep. He half considered staying in bed but he could feel the nightmare just on the edge of his consciousness, ready to strike the moment he began to nod off. And he didn't want to face it again so soon, tired as he was.

His morning routine was becoming more of an effort by the day, the simplest of tasks made increasingly difficult by the building insomnia. Somehow he managed to get himself ready for work and before long he was shambling towards the door like a zombie. At least that infernal howling had quieted again with the dawn or he might have feared to do so much as unlock it, but as it was he had no reason to suspect anything was amiss. Not until it swung open to reveal a gruesome surprise.

The smell hit him first, that unmistakeable stink of blood and death. Then came the equally repulsive sight as his eyes were drawn downwards to the source of the stench. Nausea stirred within his belly as he took in the ghoulish remains of the creature, barely recognisable as the handsome

stag it had been in life. This went far beyond the cruelty often found in nature, the violence of the poor animal's demise plain to see. Such a brutal death had rendered it ugly, transforming it into a thing of nightmares, a macabre tableau to turn even the strongest of stomachs.

Bloody rags hung down where claws had rent the flesh from the bone, jaws laid bare in a ghastly grin. A fly crawled across one sightless eye and up towards the bloody stump where the left antler used to be, while another buzzed around the jagged edge of what was once an ear. Crimson streaked vertebrae wrapped in tattered flesh was all that remained of the stag's neck. Its chest was mostly intact though it bore deep gashes across its ribs, but its lower half gaped open, a grisly vault robbed of its slimy treasures. Only the less desirable organs had been left virtually untouched. Loops of intestine had been strewn around the carcass and the stomach lay discarded by the hind legs, its contents spilt from a slit running down the middle, staining the lower legs green.

Mike's eyes picked out every detail and it was too much. He ran back inside to heave his own stomach contents into the toilet, then called in sick once he'd recovered enough from the initial shock. Between the nightmares and the howling and now this grisly find, he was too shaken up to face work that day. He could barely face what he had to do next, but he knew it would only be viler the longer he left it and so he took a swig of whiskey to help steel himself for this distasteful task, then ventured back out to clean away the scene of slaughter on his doorstep.

The young man couldn't remember ever being more grateful for a pair of gloves than he was then as he bent to pick up the loose body parts and toss them in a garbage bag. He was so intent on getting it over with as quickly as possible that he didn't notice the woman on his drive until she was stood over him.

"Looks like someone made quite the mess last night," she said.

Mike's head snapped up to find a familiar face. He took a breath to calm himself before replying "Jean? How did you know I hadn't gone into work today?"

"Afraid I'm stalking you now?" she answered with a smirk.

"No, of course not. I just - "

"I was passing by and I saw you out here," she interrupted. "Need a hand?"

"Sure, if you don't mind getting your hands dirty. I'll bring you some gloves."

"Oh, a bit of raw meat doesn't bother me. Though it seems a shame to waste good venison."

"Are you kidding me? We don't know where it's been! What if the animal that killed it was rabid? I've never seen anything like this before, even from a wolf pack or a bear."

Jean merely smiled and knelt beside him, grabbing a length of intestine in her bare hands without so much as a grimace. Mike tried to hide his revulsion but he wasn't entirely sure he'd succeeded, though Jean seemed not to notice. He was glad of the help though, and with a second pair of hands the body was soon disposed of and the gore washed away as if it had never been.

"Thanks," he said when they were done. "Do you want to come in for coffee?"

"You don't seem yourself this morning," she answered, ignoring the question. "Has the nightmare been troubling you again?"

"Gee, I wonder why. But yes, I did have the nightmare again now you mention it. I know they say it wasn't real, it can't be real, but for some reason I just can't get the image of Karen White turning into a were-wolf out of my head. I haven't slept all week!"

"I'll help you sleep."

Before he could say anything else, he found himself being led into his own home by this strange woman he was beginning to think he'd never understand. Not that they'd known each other long. He still wasn't entirely sure how she'd come to be in his life, but suddenly she'd just been there like a dark goddess summoned by his lust, and now he found himself bound to her by the very desire that had brought them together.

That desire drove them up to the bedroom. Under any other circumstances Mike would have insisted on cleaning up after handling the dead animal, but once his passion was awoken it blazed through his other emotions, burning away his disgust at the gore still tainting Jean's flesh. Those blood stained hands traced his now naked body, her soft lips working their way downwards as he lay there on the bed. Then there came a sudden pain as he felt something pierce his side, an unwelcome sensation at odds with the building pleasure flowing through him.

"Jesus, what kind of kinky shit are you into?" he asked.

Jean didn't answer, her tongue tracing the trickle of crimson fluid running across his skin. Then her mouth continued its journey downwards and his pain was soon lost in a tide of ecstasy.

Mike did fall back to sleep as Jean had promised, but she could do nothing to keep him free of the nightmare. It was the same as before – he was out in the woods on a misty night with the sound of howling echoing all around, and something was coming for him. Again he was confronted by Karen White changing into a monster just as he'd seen on the news, and again he was pulled to the floor by one of the beasts. And what he saw lying there filled him with such terror, it was no wonder he woke drenched in cold sweat every night. For there lay a ghoulish spectacle similar to the animal carcass left on his doorstep. Except this wasn't an animal. This victim had once been a man, before the life had been torn so cruelly from his vulnerable flesh. And it was not just any man.

Mike looked into eyes he'd only ever seen in a mirror, his own mutilated face staring lifelessly back at him. Tooth and claw had ravaged every inch of his double's flesh, completely obliterating all his copy had been. What it meant he didn't even want to know, but once again it had him screaming on his return to reality.

Jean woke beside him, though he took little notice of her. Those damned wolves - were back with their mournful chorus and he'd had all he could take, lack of sleep eroding any rational thoughts that might have dissuaded him from what he was about to do. Instead he let anger take hold until it became a rage such as he had never known. He fought his way free of the covers, grabbed his robe and allowed that fury to take over, driving him downstairs to the living room where he kept his hunting rifle. There was no more room for fear, a feeling of newfound power surging through him as he took hold of the gun and strode to the door, throwing it open and stepping out into a scene much like the one he'd been trapped in for so many nights past. And just like in his dreams, there was something out there with him, something more than natural wolves.

The young man stalked across his drive, eyes fixed on the dark outline of the trees across the road, straining to see anything

lurking in the shadowy woodland. A gash opened up in the clouds overhead where a beam of moonlight stabbed through, lancing down to the twilight landscape and revealing the very thing Mike searched for. He couldn't make out exactly what it was through the mist but the glimpse he got was enough to know it wasn't a wolf. He might have suspected a bear from the way it stood upright, if it hadn't been for the howling.

With a sense of triumph, he aimed down the barrel of his gun. No more would these things haunt his nights, nor disturb his sleep. Karen's noble sacrifice would not be in vain. She had tried to warn the world of what was really out there, but the world didn't want to listen. Well he had listened and he would not turn away from the truth, and he would put an end to these monsters before they could end him. All it took was the squeeze of a trigger.

A yelp of pain indicated his bullet had found its mark, the creature starting to flee. He tracked the beast's movement but just as he was about to fire again, he felt a hand grip his arm. The second shot went wild and the werewolf escaped. Mike rounded on whoever had dared to interrupt him, only to find it was Jean.

"Come back to bed."
Such was the strength of her will, any argument he might otherwise have made backed down in submission, his anger retreating to the inner darkness it was born of. That darker side to him thirsted for more blood, but Jean was leading him upstairs once again and his need to lash out at his tormentors subsided. He allowed his lover to guide him onto the mattress and laid back, the bedding still damp with the liquid essence of his fear.

"Rest," she said, settling beside him.
Mike did as she instructed, closing his eyes and letting sleep take hold once more. The nightmare didn't return, his slumber blissfully deep and uninterrupted for the first time that week. If he dreamt he had no memory of it, though some part of him was aware of howling just on the edge of that space between sleep and the waking world.

Mike yawned and rolled over to check the time, the clock by his bed declaring it to be late morning which meant he'd slept through his alarm and was already two hours late for work. He was surprisingly unconcerned by that. In fact, work didn't feel all that important that day. He felt better than he had all week, better even than before the bout of insomnia. It was amazing how much difference a good night's rest could make! And he didn't want to waste that in the office.

Jean was already up and cooking breakfast. The greasy offering tasted divine; the perfect start to a great day. Not even the thought of what the night would bring could sully his mood. But no day can last forever and with the onset of dusk came the return of the monsters, just as he knew it would.

Those unearthly cries rose up on the cool night air, and Mike's anger rose with them. The sound no longer seemed mournful then. It felt more like a challenge, one which he intended to answer with blood and violence just as the beasts appeared to have been threatening him with when they'd left their gruesome message at his front door. For what else could the stag's body have been?

The young man stormed outside to face them as he had the night before, but this time he didn't take his gun or bother with his robe, dressed only in his pyjamas. There was a strength coursing through his veins that made him feel invincible, as if he could wrestle the monsters with his bare hands. His undoing perhaps, though he wasn't thinking clearly enough to realise it. He wasn't really thinking at all, raw emotion and primal instinct guiding him into the darkness where the beasts waited.

"They are not your enemy."
"What?" he snapped, turning to find Jean in the doorway. She looked different somehow, though it took him a moment to work out why. Her eyes. They were no longer their human green.

"Don't fight it. You are one of us now. Embrace the wolf."

Her teeth were lengthening into fangs and he realised then where the pain in his side had come from during their lovemaking, though there was no trace of the bite on his skin. He felt his own canines elongating as something was awoken within him. Muscles rippled and bulged with new power until the cloth of his sleepwear started to split and he fell to his knees, his inner beast straining to break free and join its brothers and sisters. Nails were growing into vicious claws before his very eyes, and part of him yearned to give into it and run wild, to revel in the hunt. But beneath the savage urges and the rage that had taken hold of his soul, some part of him still felt fear.

"I hope you're right about him, Marsha," a male voice said from between the trees. He stepped into the moonlight, almost a man in appearance, if it hadn't been for his eyes and teeth marking him for what he truly was. "We can't afford another Karen White on our hands."

Mike looked at the woman he'd known as Jean, confusion and doubt helping to keep the wolf at bay. "Marsha?"

They ignored him and the man continued "His reaction to the meat we left for him doesn't exactly fill me with confidence."

"That was before I gave him the gift. We need to rebuild after the slaughter at the colony and there's no Dr. Waggner to hold us back now. He will adapt – it has already begun."

"Why me?" he grunted, his speech distorted by a mouth that was no longer entirely human.

"Because I like you," Marsha answered. "No more talking now. Accept the gift, and enjoy it."

He threw back his head and a roar born of pain and the beast's frustration tore its way through his thickening neck and out of jaws stretching into a muzzle. His form settled into something monstrous and the werewolf that had been Mike rose up, his pyjamas in shreds round his hind paws.

"He still has to prove himself," the man glowered.

"He will," Marsha replied.

The night's mist slid round his lupine body, cool and refreshing, caressing his fur as he ran. His limbs moved with a speed and agility he'd never known before, his paws springing over the earth with a grip and surety that was unrivalled by any kind of human footwear. And deep in his chest his great heart pounded with the thrill of the chase, strong and full of life.

All fear was gone, the terror he'd been plagued with present only in the heart of his prey now. He could hear how his quarry tired, the luckless victim's breathing turning ragged as the rush of adrenalin faded and exhaustion set in. There would be no escape.

One mighty leap and it was all over. He was on his target, jaws slathering as he bit down into soft flesh. Blood spilled into his maw and bathed his tongue in an explosion of intense taste, empowering his carnivorous hunger and inspiring more savagery. The

woman screamed as his fangs shredded her flesh but her anguished cries only drove Mike into a greater frenzy, her frail body breaking beneath his predatory might. Her screams faded to gurgles, her gurgles to silence, and she died. What was left of Mike's humanity died with her. Only the beast remained, and its need to hunt.

And so the werewolves' cries rang through the woods again that night, but they were not calling for Karen to come back to them as Mike had been foolish enough to let himself believe. He raised his snout to the sky and together they howled in defiance of the prey Dr. Waggner would have had them integrate with, the prey it was in their nature to hunt. And mankind wouldn't even see them coming. ∎

In Memory Of
Gary Phil Brandner
(May 31, 1930 – September 22, 2013)

RELEASED
(USA, Apr 10, 1981)

DIRECTOR
Joe Dante

WRITING CREDITS
Gary Brandner
(*The Howling I, II & III*)

STORY
Gary Brandner

SCREENPLAY
John Sayles,
Terence H. Winkless

CINEMATOGRAPHER
John Hora

COMPOSER
Pino Donaggio

CAST
Dee Wallace
(Karen White),
Patrick Macnee
(Dr. Waggner),
Christopher Stone
(Bill Neill),
Belinda Balaski
(Terry Fisher),
Dennis Dugan
(Chris),
Kevin McCarthy
(Fred Francis),
John Carradine
(Erle),
Slim Pickens
(Sam),
Elisabeth Brooks
(Marsha Quist),
Robert Picardo
(Eddie Quist),
Dick Miller
(Walter Paisley)

PRODUCTION COMPANY
Embassy Pictures

EDITOR
Joe Dante,
Mark Goldblatt

SPECIAL EFFECTS
Rob Bottin,
Rick Baker,
Joe Beserra,
Bill Sturgeon

RUNNING TIME
91 min

The Howling

All your nightmares are about to be transformed into one single inescapable fear!

SYNOPSIS

The Howling is the groundbreaking, darkly comic horror film from director Joe Dante (*Gremlins*) and scripted by John Sayles, loosely based on the best selling novel of the same name by Gary Brandner.

After a bizarre and near-fatal encounter with serial killer Eddie "The Mangler" Quist (Robert Picardo), television anchorwoman Karen White (Dee Wallace) is left traumatized and in dire need of a rest. Her psychiatrist sends her and her husband to The Colony, a rural retreat where select patients go to relax and participate in group therapy. However, Karen notices that The Colony appears to be populated by a number of odd characters, which together with the remote location and the strange howling she hears at night soon lead Karen to believe that something is very wrong here. When she starts looking into The Colony's affairs, the apparent resurrection of Eddie Quist soon proves to be the least of her problems...

The historiographic evolution of horror cinema has always been strongly driven by its technological developments. The horror genre has always employed diversified themes and styles to translate its cinematographic currents in wide brush strokes to spread out into different parts of the world, which communicate at a distance, influencing each other.

During the late 70s and early 80s technical evolution was at its peak and reignited an interest in cinema, setting up an entirely new style of film with varied subversive subtexts whose success was determined by its clever use of the advancement in practical effects to captivate its viewer. As a result of this evolution *The Howling* was born.

The Howling quickly became one of the most recognized horror films of the 80s amongst lycanthropy fans and came about just at the right time when Hollywood was dragging itself back

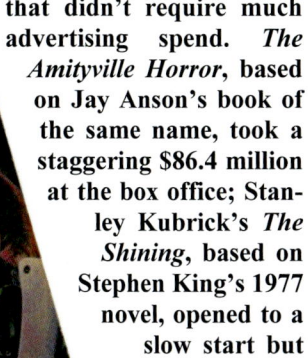

that didn't require much advertising spend. *The Amityville Horror*, based on Jay Anson's book of the same name, took a staggering $86.4 million at the box office; Stanley Kubrick's *The Shining*, based on Stephen King's 1977 novel, opened to a slow start but eventually gained momentum and became one of the biggest commercially successful films of the summer of 1980, making Warner Bros. a staggering profit. Even *Altered States*, based on a book by playwright and screenwriter Paddy Chayefsky, saw a healthy $19.8 million return, helping Hollywood studios regain the role as the undisputed kings of the cinematic global market.

1980 was a slow year for notable werewolf pictures, and not since 1941's *The Wolf Man* had there been a really successful werewolf movie, and with the advancements in special effects Lon Chaney's transformation from man into beast, which used both makeup and lap dissolve camera effects, was now dated and viewers wanted more, making *The Howling* by Gary Brandner the perfect vehicle for a cinematic adaptation. The novel, published in 1977, had captured a new style of fear and was a huge success upon its release, making it a no-brainer. AVCO Embassy Pictures, founded in the 1940s by Joseph E. Levine as Embassy Pictures Corporation, was the studio that snapped up the rights to Brandner's novel while under Robert Rehme's (*Patriot Games*) stewardship. Until 1977 AVCO Embassy Pictures had stopped making movies altogether, which eventually led to Levine resigning. When Rehme got on board he wanted AVCO Embassy to return to its former glory days when it had achieved great success with *The Graduate*, but this time around concentrate on lower-budgeted genre films, predominately horror, for the drive-in cinema market. By the end of 1980 AVCO Embassy Pictures had already began making its mark in the horror field and benefitted in part from the collapse of American International Pictures. *The Manitou* (1978), *Phantasm* (1979) and *The Fog* (1980) all had decent theatrical runs, generating enough of the green stuff to push *The Howling* into production just as

from a difficult period in history when the USA had been deeply shaken by protests against authority. This reached fever pitch after the years of the Great Depression brought on by the oil crisis, which knocked the wind out of the global economy and triggered a stock market crash, soaring inflation and high unemployment because Arab oil producers imposed an embargo to boycott America and punish the West in response to support for Israel in the Yom Kippur war against Egypt.

The Howling followed hot on the heels of *Friday the 13th*, *Maniac* and *Motel Hell*, which all fit neatly into the low-cost cinema category of films that were adapted to the new freer and juvenile film consumption market. These low-budget efforts attracted an audience that most glossy products made in the studios couldn't reach and still see a healthy return. During this period the American film industry also found success in leasing book titles that had received critical praise, as they provided the perfect platform to tap into an existing market

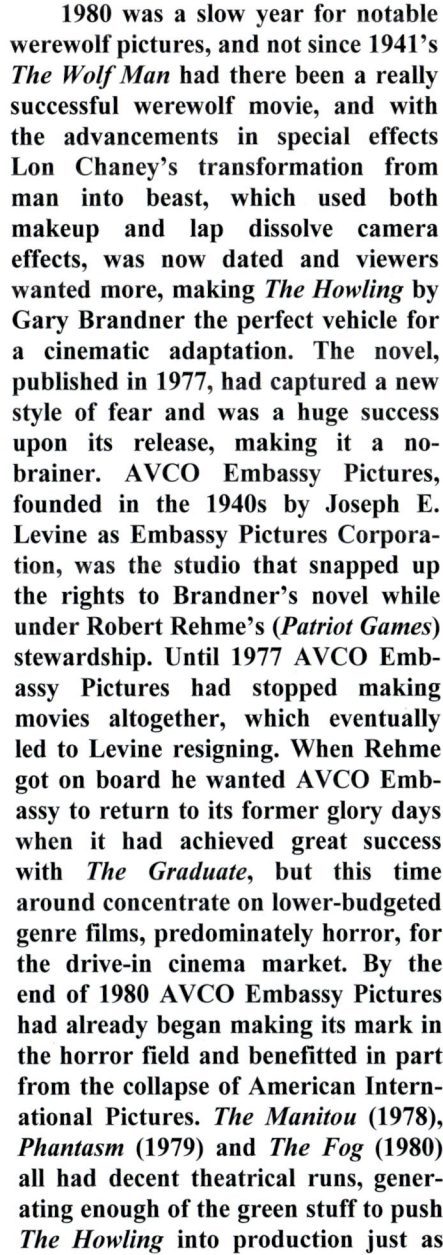

23

two other high-profile wolf-themed horror films (*Wolfen* and *An American Werewolf In London*) went into development.

AVCO Embassy Pictures originally hired *Once Upon A Time*'s Jack Conrad to direct, but Conrad's screenplay proved unsatisfactory for the studio and was more-or-less a straight-to-the-jugular text book horror film that scrimped on character development in favour of the red stuff. The finished draft that was handed into Embassy Pictures didn't fit the criteria of the studio, who demanded a high concept werewolf movie with humour, and Conrad was sent back to the drawing board to start over. Displeased with the studio's attitude and their insistence on blending terror with a chuckle as a counterbalance, after battling with them over the changes he admitted defeat and left the project.

By the time Conrad parted ways with AVCO Embassy Pictures over creative differences Terence H. Winkless (*The Nest*) had been hired to rewrite the script. Winkless, like Conrad, constructed his screenplay within the confines of Brandner's novel and stayed tightly under the shadow of *The Wolf Man*. No sooner had the completed screenplay arrived on AVCO Embassy Pictures' desk than the studio immediately began hunting for a cheap director to replace Conrad, and in his absence Joe Dante was hired, fresh from the Roger Corman-produced *Piranha*.

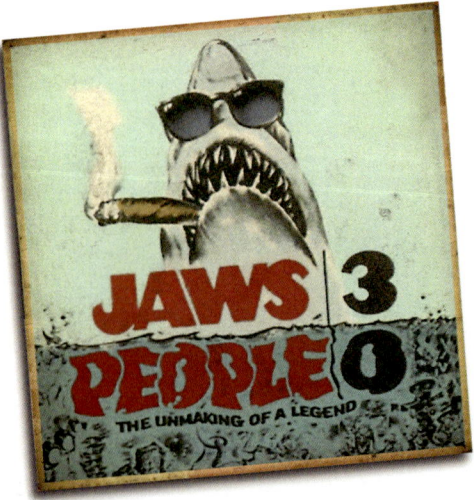

Prior to signing up for *The Howling* Dante had been offered several water-themed horror films (*Orca*), partly due to the success of *Piranha*, which had made $16 million at the box office. One of the more high profile gigs he was attached to direct was Universal Pictures' spoof *Jaws 3-D* (*Jaws 3, People 0*), which was being produced by David Brown (*Jaws 2*) and Richard Zanuck (*Compulsion*). After seeing the success of *Airplane!* the duo decided it would be a good idea to take the *Jaws* trilogy in a similar direction. With that in mind they reached out to Matty Simmons, then publisher of *National Lampoon* and the producer of *Animal House*. With Simmons on board as a producer and John Hughes (*The Breakfast Club*) along with Tod Carroll (*Clean and Sober*) hired to write the screenplay, all systems were go, but at the final hurdle the plug was pulled, freeing Dante for *The Howling*.

Dante was sent Winkless's screenplay to read and like the studio he wasn't impressed with the film's direction, feeling that the story had been told before, in many cases better. Dante was equally critical of the screenplay's source material as he felt the book wasn't all that good either, and with his motto being that he wouldn't make a movie he wouldn't go and see himself the studio allowed him to bring in John Sayles (*Piranha, Alligator*) to interject some much-needed humour into the proceedings. "One guy tried to adapt the book," Dante stated about Winkless's screenplay, "and it really wasn't working. That's when I hired John Sayles. He wrote this picture after *Piranha*. He wrote *Alligator* and *The Howling* together at the same time in the same hotel room. You'd knock on the door, and he'd ask who it was, and you'd tell him either *The Howling* or *Alligator* and he'd slip the appropriate pages under the door."

It was Dante's first collaboration with

longtime producer Michael Finnell (*Gremlins*), who gave Dante the chance to not only play in the sandbox of a horror subgenre he obviously cared a great deal for, but also to resurrect it for a new generation, one with an acute awareness of the mythos of monster movies and all the various clichés that went along with it. With Sayles on board *The Howling* was already shaping up to be something very unique. When hired to rewrite *The Howling* Sayles was already in the midst of writing the screenplay for Lewis Teague's *Alligator*, another high concept horror film that followed a police officer and a reptile expert on their hunt for a giant murderous sewer alligator that had begun attacking residents after escaping from its dwellings. Like *The Howling*, *Alligator* was intentionally satirizing its genre, and often scenes Sayles had written for *The Howling* ended up in *Alligator* and vice versa. Sayles, who had collaborated with Dante on the tongue-in-cheek horror *Piranha*, knew textually what Dante was looking for, so he kept *The Howling*'s screenplay focused on similar self-aware, satirical aspects that had made *Piranha* such a critical hit that it even received praise from Steven Spielberg, who commented that Dante's film and Sayles' script was one of "the best of the *Jaws* ripoffs".

Sayles wrote *The Howling* screenplay while travelling back and forth from New York to Los Angeles and immediately began by throwing out almost the entire work Winkless had done. Sayles carefully withheld any notion of the supernatural at the beginning of his screenplay, focusing on all-too-human monstrousness before eventually settling on that universal creature that combines both monster and human in hybrid form. The completed script had only vague resemblance to Brandner's novel and after many attempts at tweaking Winkless's screenplay Dante and Sayles made the decision to completely remodel what was on paper, building on the characters and their situations and appropriating the book for screen, replacing character names with those of the directors of werewolf movies and including entirely celluloid-based mythology. They crafted a psychological thriller with an amnesiac heroine who seeks refuge in a Colony (a satire of the then-popular Self Help movement) to try and unlock her repressed memories, and it was only then that Sayles' script unwittingly transformed into a full-blown werewolf movie. When Brandner got wind of what was happening to his labour of love he was infuriated by Dante and Sayles' direction, which left a bitter taste in the best-selling author's mouth. Brandner wasn't overly fond of the screenplay's endearing self-aware sense of humour, and felt it removed the dread-laced plot he crafted that had thrilled readers worldwide. In fact, he felt the script had simply parodied his source material and lacked his well-constructed plot, and much like Dante's previous film (*Piranha*) *The Howling* had simply become a "series of gags" and references to "bad movies." This didn't deter Dante or Sayles and they pressed on with the project. To make sure Sayles was on hand for any last minute script revisions during the making of the film Dante had Sayles cleverly orchestrate a minor yet significant role for himself within the film. Dante was aware that, unless Sayles was on the payroll as an actor, AVCO Embassy Pictures wouldn't allocate a budget for him to fly to and from location, so Sayles was given the role of Morgue Attendant, which appeased the studio and gave them reason to cough up Sayles' travel and accommodation expenses. "If you hire him as an actor," Dante said, "you can make a case for it."

The Howling's casting was handled by Susan Arnold (*The Clonus Horror*) and Judith Weiner (*Sparkle*), who had cast *Piranha* for Dante, and again they decided to cast recognizable character actors such as John Carradine (*The Vampires*), Kenneth Tobey (*Rage*), Dick Miller (*New York, New York*) and Slim Pickens (*Christmas Mountain*) alongside familiar genre stars that were household names among horror fans – Belinda Balaski (*Black Eye*) and Kevin McCarthy (*Invasion of the Body Snatchers*). Balaski was a Dante favourite because of her patience on *Piranha* when it came to her prosthetic latex appliances. "Balaski was beyond tolerant," Dante stated. Other recognizable horror cameos went to set

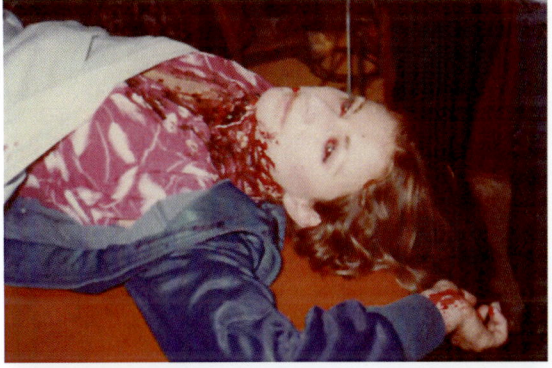

designer Robert A. Burns (*The Texas Chainsaw Massacre*), who had previously crossed paths with Dee Wallace on *The Hills Have Eyes*, Forrest J. Ackerman, who appeared for a brief moment in the occult bookstore run by Miller, clutching a copy of his own magazine *Famous Monsters of Filmland* and Roger Corman, whose brief but lingering appearance at the beginning of *The Howling* was of an impatient man waiting for Dee Wallace (*Cujo*) to finish her call in a phone booth situated in a gritty urban expanse where adult films and B-movies played next door to each other.

Miller was less enthusiastic about his role in *The Howling*. He said he received a call out of the blue and was told there was a day's work for him on the film if he wanted it. "That's it?" he replied. It was then explained to him that he didn't look the part for any of the roles and he certainly didn't fit the bill as a werewolf. After a few minutes of pondering over the job offer he responded, "I'll take it!" The character Walter Paisley (Bookstore Owner) would later become Miller's favourite role and he would go on to star in a further 13 Joe Dante movies including *Gremlins*, *Gremlins 2: The New Batch*, *Small Soldiers* and *Burying the Ex*.

During the casting process Las Vegas porn star Annette Haven was suggested for the role of Marsha Quist, which eventually went to Elisabeth Brooks (*Deep Space*). Haven, who was considered one of the legendary porn stars of her decade, was reached out to on numerous occasions but the *Dracula Sucks* star declined the offer because she was opposed to the screenplay's violent content. Robert Picardo (*976-EVIL*) also took some convincing to sign on the dotted line. Arnold admired Picardo, who had graduated from Yale with a Bachelor's degree in Drama, and she desperately wanted to sign him up for the lead villain of the piece. At the time he was cast in his feature film debut (*The Howling*) as Eddie Quist he had just completed a successful and rewarding stint on Broadway and had no plans for swapping the stage for the big screen. But after some persuasive negotiations and a few dangled carrots Picardo finally agreed to take on the role.

Dee Wallace was hired early on to play Karen White. The *Hills Have Eyes* actress negotiated hard when it came to the film's nudity and forced the studio's hand to re-adjust several scenes to accommodate her 'no nudity' clause in her contract. "I had some of the gratuitous nudity removed from some of the scenes," Wallace stated, "but I really thought it was well written and said a sound statement on the dark side of human nature." Wallace wasn't fond of gratuitous nudity in cinema and later turned down the offer of returning to the franchise in *The Howling II*. "They asked me if I was interested," she stated, "and I kind of said, 'I don't do any material that borders on pornography yet.'"

With Wallace hired the studio now only had the role of Wallace's on-screen husband, Bill Neill, to fill. During a telephone conversation between Wallace and Executive Producer Daniel H. Blatt (*Bloody Birthday*) the issue of finding a "really sexy, virile man with vulnerability" to play him came up in conversation. Wallace immediately suggested Christopher Stone (*CHiPs*), to whom she had recently become engaged. "You know, I worked with this guy on *CHiPs* and he's exactly like what you just described," Wallace recalled.

Within days of the telephone conversation Blatt had Arnold and Weiner headhunt Stone to bring him in for an audition. Blatt loved Stone's audition and personally made the call to him to offer him the role, but Wallace answered the phone. Slightly confused, he apologized to Wallace and told

her he had recently called Stone in for an audition and was trying to get hold of him to offer him the role and must have dialled her number by mistake. Wallace replied, "Yeah, I know. I'm engaged to him." This was followed by a lengthy silence before Blatt responded, "Aw, shit. You guys are gonna gang up on me!"

With the cast and crew all in place the next logical step was to find a SFX artist up to the job of bringing the film's creatures from the script's pages to life. Joe and the film's producers wanted nothing but the best, their end goal being to blow the audience away with state-of-the-art transformation never before seen on the big screen, and if they couldn't achieve their goal and break the mould they didn't want to make the film at all, a sentiment also shared by Rob Bottin (*The Witches of Eastwick*), who was just 21 at the time *The Howling* began filming.

Rick Baker (*Cursed*), who retired from the motion picture industry in 2015, was the first artist to be hired to create *The Howling*'s creatures. "Joe Dante and Mike Finnell called me," Baker recalled. "Mike had sent me the paperback novel, and they told me they were going to make a picture. Now, John Landis had been talking to me about doing *An American Werewolf in London* for ten years. We had talked about it – there were a couple of times when it seemed it might happen, but it didn't."

Dante and Finnell explained to Baker that, while the budget was extremely tight, he could have all the creative freedom in the world. "And that's very appealing to me," he added. "I spoke to Landis, and he said that we were definitely going to go ahead on *American Werewolf* – but I had heard that before."

Baker felt split down the middle and devised a solution to the issue. He remained as a designer and consultant and first port of contact on *The Howling* and handed his protegé Rob Bottin the actual creature effects. Bottin had begun his career fairly early in life at the age 14 when he mailed his idol (Rick Baker) a letter containing a picture he drew with the hope of getting the SFX mogul's autograph in return. But Baker, being Baker, did one better and offered instead to hire Bottin as his personal apprentice. Prior to *The Howling* the El Monte-born SFX artist had worked on the 1976 *King Kong* remake before going on to team up with Dante on the fish-out-of-water horror/comedy *Piranha*, so Dante knew what to expected from the SFX guru. "They'd worked with Rob before, on *Piranha*," said Baker, "so I suggested that I act as designer and supervising consultant and let Rob do the actual work. I don't think they were as aware of Rob's abilities as they were of mine at the time, so that made them feel better." One of the biggest issues Bottin faced was the film's miniscule budget he was given to create all the film's SFX.

Shot in just 28 days, the film faced several uphill battles. Dante, who at that point had never experienced working with a method actor, was taken aback by Wallace's work ethic. Wallace was both fragile and unwilling to rehearse her scenes prior to shooting, a polar opposite to Stone, who liked to know exactly what he was doing, where he was standing and how the scene was going to be portrayed and shot before the director called "Action". Not only did Wallace's approach to filming confuse Dante to begin with but the iconic actress had a particular aversion to violence, so filming a scene such as the one where her character Karen is positioned facing the screen in a dark porno booth as a grisly snuff film played while she had her back to Eddie so neither can see the other as he gradually transformed didn't come easy. Wallace's insistence to live in the character's moment only heightened on-set tension and often made it difficult for Dante to switch up scenes as it would take Wallace several hours to come down after filming a scene that involved expressing her primal fear.

Robert Picardo, like Wallace, found the shoot testing on a professional level and physical. He would turn up to set prepared and ready to film but would have to sit for hours in the make-up chair having latex applied to his face. One day Bottin, who was a perfectionist in every sense of the word,

took Picardo to the make-up room while Dante and the crew prepared the scene. Several hours later Bottin was still applying latex to the actor's face. Picardo became despondent and agitated at the process and when the appliance was finally ready to go before camera Dante was unable to film as the SAG talent had to leave because they were subject to restrictions on work hours, even though the film was non-union. Picardo became furious, and while having the latex removed he began to regret signing up for the project, and even considered throwing in the towel. The following day he once again had to go through the same monotonous process.

With his SFX applied Picardo eventually went before the camera lens and filmed one of cinema's most jaw-dropping, bone-breakingly intense transformations ever to grace celluloid. Bottin had created various air bladders under Picardo's latex facial applications to give the illusion of an internal transformation, an idea devised by make-up artist Dick Smith (*The Exorcist*) for the transformation sequences in *Altered States*. As well as the bladders placed under Picardo's forehead, cheeks and neck they were additionally added to the chest, shoulders and arms and concealed with layer upon layer of make-up appliances. The finished look included contact lenses and prosthetic teeth. The effect of Eddie's nails growing into claws was achieved with a hollow insert hand with cable-controlled nails that could slowly spring into action, a technique, inspired by stiletto blades. The inflatable air bladder tubing, however, proved difficult for the actor when the tubes were filled to capacity with air as the bladders around his neck would gradually close the actor's throat, and during one take Picardo risked suffocation when the bladder on his neck over-inflated before exploding. Once Picardo had completed his scenes he was replaced by several sculpted heads known as the 'Change-o-Heads'. These were developed through an all-day casting session with the actor. Bottin made five full-head casts and also several face studies. Rather than making the wolf on Picardo's face, Bottin made it from his own face. "That may sound like the same thing, but I was taking Bob's features and distorting them, making them animalistic," Bottin said of the process. "I looked for characteristics in his face that could be frightening to me and exaggerated them. I think we came up with a really weird look."

The Change-o-Heads were built with techniques first experimented with on *Tanya's Island*, a film directed by Alfred Sole, and refined for *The Howling*. The animatronics and their mechanical designs were devised by Bottin and Doug Beswick (*King Kong Lives*). Complex mechanical assemblies shifted parts of the skull, altering its appearance in predetermined areas, such as by elongating the jaw. A total of three 'Change-o-Heads' were devised to represent the progressive stages of transformation, each capable of up to 15 different actions to fit with Dante's filming frame rates so he could avoid using dissolves. This was so the viewer could see the transformation from start to finish without too many cuts being made, producing a transformation that appears to be organic. Dante began shooting the scene at 24 frames per second, which was normal speed, but then would drop it and speed it up according to the transformation. Shooting in this way also helped to hide any minor imperfections that were visible.

When it came time to shoot Belinda Balaski's death, the werewolf the crew had planned to use was incomplete and still sitting in the workshop gathering dust due to running out of budget, something which hindered another scene in the movie between Christopher Stone and Elisabeth Brooks. Dante

once again pressed on and shot around the problem by using what he had available. When the scene was in the can he returned to AVCO Embassy Pictures and asked for more money, which they agreed to after seeing the dailies. Several months after putting tools down the cast and crew return to shoot Balaski's confrontation with the werewolf, which was shot in two parts – one using a puppet and the second a man in a suit to achieve the overall look Dante desired. The finished scene provided one of the best on-screen metamorphoses and fully-fledged werewolves in history of the horror genre until that point.

Stone and Brooks' sex scene, however, was considered a low point for the film! The scene hit problems from the get go, with Wallace finding the idea of her husband-to-be becoming intimate with another uncomfortable. Eventually, after several discussions about the scene and how it would be shot, which Wallace had already had toned down, all parties involved felt it was best that Wallace wasn't on set on the day of the shoot. When it came to filming the scene Stone had difficulty with the lengthy make-up process. The contact lenses were unpleasant and Stone found them painful to wear, the drool-inducing retracting fangs were also vexatious. The transformation utilized in the sequences employed similar techniques that were applied to Picardo. Bottin achieved the drool-inducing retracting fangs by using a built-in prosthetic device hidden within Stone's and Brooks' mouths. A compact lever was then concealed by a palette piece, with the tongue control in turn covered by the actor's snarl, which operated a bar that elongated the teeth accordingly. The very structure of the prosthetic meant that it could only be shot at certain angles to achieve the desired effect on screen. The scene furthermore called for Stone and Brooks to transform into full lycan form, but this proved an issue due to time and financial constraints. With the partial metamorphosis sequences in the can Dante resolved the problem by using animated silhouettes for the final stages of the transformation, employing replacement cel animation by Pete Kuran (*Conan the Barbarian*) for the scene, which deviates in tone from the rest of the film.

When it came to filming the film's climactic burning barn scenes, Dante and the crew were all concerned that they couldn't afford enough full-sized werewolves on the set to really suggest the appearance of a whole werewolf colony going up in flames, so they made the unwise decision to use stop-motion. To achieve the visuals producer Michael Finnell (*Teaching Mrs. Tingle*) reached out to animator David W. Allen (*Dolls*). Finnell outlined the basic parameters of what Dante was looking for with the stop-motion werewolves and told him how, during principal photography, two full werewolf suits were built, along with an insert animatronic head and insert arms, but the results were visually unsatisfying and the werewolves resembled bears rather than wolves. Allen was shown the life-sized animatronic werewolf rod puppet, which had a wide range of motions, but it was discarded and never used.

Allen, satisfied he could achieve the look they desired, went away and created an in-proportion puppet using the rod puppet as a base for the stop-motion werewolves. He applied some creative changes to the design by pinching in the werewolf's waist like a greyhound, accentuating the chest area and reducing the shoulders. The werewolf puppets were sculpted by Roger Dicken (*2001: A Space Odyssey*). Allen and Ernie Farino (*Critters*) built the armatures using components recycled from the *Davey and Goliath* TV series. Three long stop-motion sequences were animated. Allen took three shots of the stop-motion creatures, each of which was cut into several more shots, but sadly it became apparent when they viewed the finished scenes that the stop-motion werewolves didn't fit with the rest of the live-action footage. The werewolves themselves looked different to the final werewolf design used in the reshoots, and the way the scenes were lit conflicted with Director of Photography John Hora's (*Eerie, Indiana*) work on the film. Allen's footage included one very complicated shot that opened with a moving camera and ended on a static shot. While executed with style, once cut into the movie it felt out of place, almost tacked on from an entirely different movie. Eventually the decision was made to cut the stop-motion almost entirely, using only the segment that had the werewolves who had escaped the barn howling up at the full moon after

Due to the fact that Wallace wasn't in favour of looking like the other werewolves in the movie Bottin appeased the actress and created a Bambi-esque design to reflect the fact that Karen had rejected werewolf society and wanted to resist her newfound instincts.

Karen's escape. The single stop-motion shot that survived the final edit is only a fleeting moment and a dissolve was added to keep the proceedings rolling.

For *The Howling*'s score Dante turned for the second time in his career to Pino Donaggio (*Death Proof*), after working with him on *Piranha*. Donaggio, who has since gone on to become one of the most successful Italian composers to amass a healthy discography outside of his native Italy, was still in the formative years of his career, though he had scored a few films of note by then (*Carrie, Beyond Evil*). Dante wanted to enhance *The Howling* with a forebodingly sinister and romantically erotic sound and felt Donaggio was the perfect man for the job. The studio flew Donaggio in from Italy and because of his inability to speak English and Dante not being able to speak Italian, Paul Bartel (*Death Race 2000*) was brought in to speak Spanish because Pino

also spoke a little Spanish. With the translator in tow they played the movie to Donaggio, and Bartel in Spanish would let Donaggio know where the music would start and where it would stop. With a brief outline of what Dante wanted Donaggio flew back to Italy where he wrote the film's music, then mailed the complete score back to American soil with a note of where the music was supposed to start and stop. Donaggio's method of scoring music was unusual to say the least, but his use of organ-based sounds supported by an orchestral texture with melodic woodwind leading the way fitted perfectly, and everyone was pleased with his work.

One day before the film went to print Dante once again picked up the camera to film Wallace's transformation – a late addition to the film. Due to the fact that Wallace wasn't in favour of looking like the other werewolves in the movie Bottin appeased the actress and created a Bambi-esque design to reflect the fact that Karen had rejected werewolf society and wanted to resist her newfound instincts. The overall look pleased Dante and the cameras rolled for one last time with a single mid-transformation animatronic head. The climax was shot completely in close-up in Dante's office.

Further cuts were made to the film after test screenings commenced and it became apparent to Dante that numerous scenes did not fit with the rest of the live-action footage. One specific deleted scene involved a full-size werewolf being shot out of the barn during the inferno. The so-called rocket werewolf was cut due to a visible vapour trail being left behind and the results were deemed comical. A scene where Karen (Wallace) returned to her cabin looking for Bill (Stone) before getting into her car was left on the cutting room floor because the stop-motion wolf that appears from behind a tree as Karen runs off screen didn't sit right with viewers. "People were coming up to me and asking what picture the neat stop-motion footage came from," Dante said of the test screening. "There was nothing wrong with those shots; it was just that the werewolves moved differently – like in a Ray Harryhausen (*Clash of the Titans*) film where they cut from a stop-motion creature to a full-size live-action shot." Several dialogue scenes were additionally trimmed to tighten up the film's running time before *The Howling* was released on April 10th 1981. The film's advertising campaign peddled *The Howling* as a thriller/slasher because werewolf movies had by that point lost their pop-culture bite with cinemagoers.

The campaign for *The Howling* worked well considering the up-and-coming cinematic slate of horror films that were set to Follow – *The Burning, Halloween II, My Bloody Valentine, The Prowler* and *Final Exam*. Slasher films were at their height of popularity when *The Howling* hit cinemas, but Bottin's work blew the world away in the effects department and Sayles' black-as-ink comedy gave the film an edge that other horror films at that time lacked. *The Howling* went on to rake in nearly $18 million at the box office, but it was *An American Werewolf*

in London that would eventually eclipse Joe Dante's cult classic. Prior to the release of *An American Werewolf in London* another werewolf movie found its way onto the big screen – an adaptation of Whitley Strieber's 1978 novel of the same name, *Wolfen*. The film failed to make an impact and is mostly forgotten. Wolfen took $10.6 million upon its release and, while it received generally positive reviews from critics for its frightening content, *The Howling* was acknowledged as the modern-day practical effects master in the wolf stakes up until that point.

An American Werewolf in London was released a mere four months after *The Howling*, and roared onto the big screen pulling the sheepskin rug from beneath its competitor, taking a staggering $30 million at the box office and trumping *The Howling* in a critical landslide, eventually winning an Academy Award for Best Makeup and Hairstyling.

But while *An American Werewolf in London* has gone on to be considered the benchmark of

Bottin's work blew the world away in the effects department and Sayles' black-as-ink comedy gave the film an edge that other horror films at that time lacked.

practical FX perfection and box office gold it's *The Howling*'s kooky humour by Sayles and Dante's wicked direction and Dee Wallace's performance as Karen White that makes *The Howling* reign supreme over *An American Werewolf in London*. Pitting both films toe-to-toe probably wouldn't find you a definitive champion, but it sure does make for a hell of a mini-movie marathon.

On August 28th 1985 *Howling II: Your Sister Is a Werewolf* finally made its way onto the silver screen, and while *The Howling* was a huge success for AVCO Embassy Pictures, Robert Rehme had left the company and the studio decided not to exercise their sequel rights and the series was taken over by Hemdale Film (*The Terminator*). ∎

1.

The Dee Wallace interview

Dee Wallace is one of the Horror genre's most powerful actresses, dominating the screen with a performance that commands all of the viewer's attention, no matter who shares her screen time. With a résumé that spans four plus decades, with roles in over ninety feature films including *Critters*, *ET* and *Cujo*, Wallace continues to keep herself busy acting and also finding tranquility in helping others as a public speaker, author and host of a weekly radio show titled *Conscious Creation*.

The Howling was Wallace's earliest feature film, a relentless horror that aimed for the jugular in every sense of the word. In her own words Dee Wallace opens up about *The Howling*'s on-screen nudity, her raw energy and seeing the movie for the very first time!

DEE WALLACE

SIGNING ON THE DOTTED LINE FOR *THE HOWLING*:
I have to like the script and the character. I always look for an arc to play, and whether my energy resonates with the character. Ha! And it was the lead in a studio film with a good director at the beginning of my career! No-brainer!

I had some of the gratuitous nudity removed from some of the scenes, but I really thought it was well written and said a sound statement on the dark side of human nature.

ON THE CASTING OF CHRISTOPHER STONE:
I had just gotten engaged to Christopher and I got this part. Dan Blatt calls me and says, "Well, Dee, it's going really great. We've got a great cast for you, but we can't find a guy for your husband." Now, I had read the script. Why this did not occur to me… Maybe it was just that I didn't think that they'd listen to me. But I said, "Well, what exactly are you looking for, Dan?" And he said, "Well, you know, a really sexy, virile man with vulnerability." Well, within 10 seconds, my mind put together this whole scenario: "If you suggest Chris right now, they're never going to do that, because they know you're an item, and they're gonna be afraid to hire both of you." So I said, "You know, I worked with this guy on *CHiPs*, and he's exactly like what you just described: Christopher Smith? Stone? Something like that." So they went out and they found him and brought him in to audition, and he got the part.

The next day after he got the part, the

phone rings and I pick it up, and Dan goes, "Dee?" I said, "Hi, Dan!" And he said, "I... I'm sorry, I must've called the wrong number. But you know that guy you suggested? Well, we found him, we brought him in, and we booked him." I said, "Yeah, I know. I'm engaged to him." And there was this very very long pause. And then he went, "Aw, shit." [Laughs.] He said, "You guys are gonna gang up on me!" "No, Dan, we're not gonna gang up on you." And by the end of the picture, he was saying, "Thank god Chris was here and he can handle her."

So it turned out to be a really, really positive thing for all of us, and we all became really close friends.

ON HORROR FINDING HER:
I did not go looking for them, they found me and I just happened to be a really great screamer and crier. I was also able to play the subtleties of a really connected character and the Horror films that I participated in were all really good attributes to have. I like working in them. I think that Horror fans are the best fans in the world. I have done a lot of other movies of the week, and a lot of other films that are not in the Horror genre, and actually some of them were in the Comedy genre. I love my Horror fans. I think they are some of the best people in the world.

ON PREPARING FOR HER *THE HOWLING* ROLE:
I didn't. I have a minor in journalism. I worked on the school newspaper and my brother was a journalist for a ton of his life. If I have to learn something really, really technical, I will study and break it down. My method of acting is more being more in the moment and just being real and kind of channelling the character. So I don't work on my part unless it is something technical that I really need to learn.

ON DEALING WITH *THE HOWLING*'S NUDITY:
Not my role, but Christopher's! I had to deal with how I was going to deal with his nude scene and be a professional about it!

ON *THE HOWLING* SEQUELS AND NOT REPRISING HER ROLE IN *HOWLING II*:
The classy elements of one were largely lost, I thought. Too much gratuitous nudity. They asked me if I was interested (*The Howling II*), and I kind of said, "I don't do any material that borders on pornography yet." I just didn't think that it was on par at all – the script, I'm talking about – with the original *Howling*.

THE HOWLING'S ON-SCREEN RAW

EMOTION:
I get my energy really high and allow the character to swallow me up. That's the ride!

Some roles call for you to strike a much greater emotional curve than others, but basically my technique is one of the easiest acting techniques that you can use, once you master it. It's all based on very high energy and making it all about the other person and *not* coming in with any ideas. I've been working this way for thirty years and now Clint Eastwood *always* shoots the rehearsal and Meryl Streep doesn't rehearse now, and it's like the new thing. Charles Conrad was a proponent of that back in the eighties – he was my mentor.

ON LEAVING THE CHARACTER ON THE SET:
I studied with Charles Conrad, who is my mentor. High energy, throw your energy, put all the focus outside yourself, and channel. It's a total high.

Some of them (characters) go home with you. Even after. I am better now, but before I didn't always know how to get back to me.

Now I do deep knee bends, run my hands up my body to raise energy,

"They asked me if I was interested (The Howling II), and I kind of said, "I don't do any material that borders on pornography yet." I just didn't think that it was on par at all – the script, I'm talking about – with the original Howling."

shake them, pray and GO!

JOE DANTE AND THE ON-SET HOWLING FAMILY:
Joe Dante is an amazing director. He knows exactly what he wants, but also gives you the freedom to explore and create. That movie would not be half the movie it is if we hadn't had Joe Dante. He paid for all the commercials that are in there himself. He was instrumental in bringing in the names of characters from a lot of the old werewolf movies. He just added so much in there for the true horror fan.

It was a family affair, from the beginning to the end. It was a family unit coming together to make a great piece of work with a lot of limitations. And we did, and it is.

FILMING THE HOWLING:
We worked long hours, six days a week. But really satisfied. I felt like I did some good work, with good people, and got to share it with my fiancé. Nice life.

ON THE HOWLING'S ORIGINAL ENDING:
There was too much nudity. There was way too much.

Our producer, Dan Blatt, came to the set and agreed (to tone it down). I love that man!

ON HER FAVOURITE AND LEAST FAVOURITE SCENE:
I thought the tub scene was fun, with all the iconic film actors around me.

Any scene with a gun. I hate them. I'm scared to use them. Freaks me out.

FILMING THE INFAMOUS WEREWOLF SCENE:
This'll be an interesting story because they didn't have anything for me to react to in the big transformation. They took the transformation weeks after I filmed that. What I was acting with was air and Joe Dante's voice walking me through it.

The easiest understanding I can give you is…kids see monsters coming out of their closets all the time. That's really all we're doing – we're just getting ourselves to an energetic pitch where we really can believe that there's something there in front of us. We're taking ourselves into that place that children take themselves, which is kind of giving up control and letting yourself go into that imaginary place where it's there – whether it's there or not.

ON HER CHARACTER'S TRANSFORMATION:
My little Bambi werewolf. Actually that's an animatronics in there. I was up shooting *Cujo* and they called to ask if it was okay to show my character as a werewolf because they had in my contract that it wouldn't be. I okayed it, but asked Joe if they could make her a little more vulnerable because she fought so hard against it and that's what they came up with, that little Bambi werewolf.

ON SEEING THE MOVIE FOR THE FIRST TIME:
I was whooping and clapping. And awestruck at the special effects.

I just rewatched it. Loved it all over again. It is a commentary on the battle between the dark side of human nature and the truth that we are love. With fur.

ON A POSSIBLE REMAKE:
Go ahead and try. CGI just ain't the same. ■

RELEASED
(USA, Aug 28, 1985)

DIRECTOR
Philippe Mora

WRITING CREDITS
Gary Brandner
(*The Howling I, II & III*)

STORY
Gary Brandner

SCREENPLAY
Gary Brandner,
Robert Sarno

CINEMATOGRAPHER
Geoffrey Stephenson

COMPOSER
Steve Parsons

CAST
Christopher Lee
(Stefan Crosscoe),
Annie McEnroe
(Jenny Templeton),
Reb Brown
(Ben White),
Marsha A.
Hunt (Mariana),
Judd Omen (Vlad),
Sybil Danning
(Stirba)

PRODUCTION COMPANY
Hemdale,
Cinema '84/Greenberg Brothers Partnership

EDITOR
Charles Bornstein

SPECIAL EFFECTS
Cosmekinetics Inc.,
Steve Johnson

RUNNING TIME
91 min

Howling II:
Your Sister Is a Werewolf

The Rocking, Shocking, New Wave of Horror!

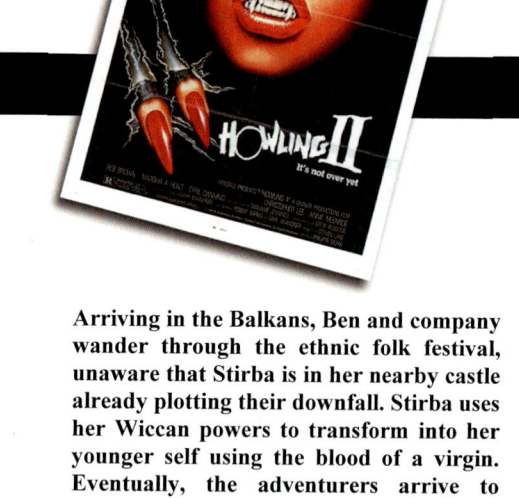

SYNOPSIS

Ben White (Reb Brown) attends the funeral of his sister, journalist Karen White, who had died during a live news broadcast at the hand of fellow journalist Chris Halloran. Ben meets Jenny Templeton (Annie McEnroe), one of Karen's colleagues, and Stefan Crosscoe (Christopher Lee), a mysterious interloper who tells him his sister is now a werewolf of the night. Providing videotaped evidence of the transformation Crosscoe returns to the chapel of rest to destroy Karen as her undead body rises from the grave. After Ben sees the dark forces at work with his own eyes Crosscoe convinces him and Jenny to accompany him to Transylvania to battle Stirba (Sybil Danning), an immortal werewolf queen. Along the way the wayward trio encounter Mariana (Marsha Hunt), a lusty werewolf siren, and her minion, Erle (Ferdy Mayne).

Arriving in the Balkans, Ben and company wander through the ethnic folk festival, unaware that Stirba is in her nearby castle already plotting their downfall. Stirba uses her Wiccan powers to transform into her younger self using the blood of a virgin. Eventually, the adventurers arrive to battle Stirba in an assault in which they must face her furry followers, disguised dwarves, mutilated priests and supernatural parasites in a fight to the death!

This is the rocking, shocking, new wave of horror, *Howling II*, twice the terror, twice the torment – can you howl for it?

Christopher Lee, Sybil Danning, bestiality, gore, Gothic architecture, it can only mean one thing; we are talking about *Howling II: Stirba – Werewolf Bitch*!

After the success of Joe Dante's 1981 film, Hemdale Film Corporation decided it was about time for a sequel. The production company behind *Return of the Living Dead* and *The Terminator* invited Gary Brandner to the table after Brandner openly crucified John Sayles' (*Piranha*) take on his 1977 novel.

The original draft Gary submitted was built around the second book in the series released in 1979 (later republished as *Return of the Howling*) and, as he put it, "My first draft was lovingly true to the book."

During the first story meeting the producers, John Daly (*Platoon*) and Steven A. Lane (*Lawnmower Man 2: Beyond Cyberspace*), expressed that, while they liked the story, it wasn't what they envisioned, and Steven A. Lane also wanted a part for his friend Fernando Rey (*The Hit*).

Dutifully, yet grudgingly, Gary went home and wrote in the veteran actor. During the follow-up meeting to review the new draft another issue arose that left a bitter taste in the author's mouth:

the money was now coming from Spaniards, and the story needed to take place in Spain. And Fernando Rey had bailed out.

Gary headed back to bulk up the plot and move his synopsis to Spain, but Steven A. Lane received news that the Spanish investor had pulled out, leaving the only option to shoot on the cheap in Yugoslavia. When the bad news reached Brandner he took the same road as the others and left the project, using *The Brain Eaters* (book) contract and its pending deadline as his valid excuse to bail.

Robert Sarno (*Decoy*) took over screenwriting duties, and the plot diverted completely from previous drafts submitted for consideration. Sarno's story follows Ben White's journey to discover who murdered his sister, Karen. With the help of werewolf hunter Stefan Crosscoe and reporter Jenny Templeton they head to Transylvania, where they are confronted by disguised dwarves, mutilated priests and supernatural parasites before they take on the immortal werewolf queen Stirba.

With the script complete, locations locked and a $2 million budget in the bag, casting began under the keen eye of Rebecca Howard, best known for her work on ITV's *The Bill*.

Philippe Mora was hired as the film's director because the Mora family had been closely associated with many of the most prominent artists and writers of the era, including the members of the now-legendary Heide Circle. This gave the film the image of being something more sophisticated than it actually was on paper. Before *Howling II* Mora's body of work included *Trouble in Molopolis*, *Mad Dog Morgan*, *The Beast* and *A Breed Apart*.

First signs of problems that would continue throughout the filming began when they arrived in Prague to discover the cast and crew were not allowed phones, photocopiers or the usual communication tools. Instead of phones they were given six guys on bicycles running around the set and studio to pass on any vital information.

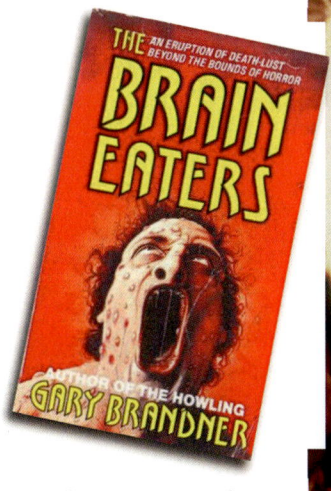

An innocent casting call by Mora looking for "punks" descended into chaos after an advert placed in the local Czech Republic paper resulted in a thousand individuals arriving. The results were catastrophic, and both the police and the military were called, causing mayhem for all involved. Philippe Mora was instructed by an army colonel, "You can finish shooting the scene, but they'll have to leave in groups of no more than three."

Things eased up when filming at Barrandov Studios (*The Young Indiana Jones Chronicles* was filmed here in 1992 and Michael Cohn used the same studio for *Snow White: A Tale of Terror*), but not for long. Difficulties arose in the form of Mora's government-assigned assistant director, Tony Cech, who knew nothing of filmmaking but gradually picked things up as he went along, and later from the studio back home.

MUSIC: THEME SONG

With *The Howling*'s 1981 score (Pino Donaggio, *Trauma*) following a very traditional pattern it was no surprise that *Howling II*'s producers, which included *Return of The Living Dead*'s Grahame Jennings, would want to put their own unique stamp on the series. Composer Stephen W. Parsons (*The Marsupials: The Howling III*) was drafted to compose, while the rest of the score was primarily provided by a pop band called Babel (Chris Pye, Steve Parsons & Simon Etchell). Babel makes two appearances in the film to perform the title track Howling, which includes an appearance during the closing credits. The vinyl album released in Germany in 1986 by Filmtrax includes additional music by Robert Randles.

TRACK LISTING

1. Wolf suite 1 (01:33)
2. Howling theme (03:07)
3. Your sister is a werewolf (04:15)
4. Wolf suite 2 (00:41)
5. Lovers sacrifice (03:29)
6. Howling club mix (04:10)
7. Wolf suite 3 (00:38)
8. Death dwarf (01:53)
9. Howling splatter mix (04:36)
10. Gotterdammerung (06:40)
11. Howling instrumental (02:40)
12. Wolf suite 4 (00:17)

This wasn't even taking into account the oppressive atmosphere brought on by the lurking KGB spies huddled in each corner of the set. Even Sybil Danning and Christopher Lee couldn't escape the scrutiny of the KGB. One evening, while they were having a light bite to eat, Danning noticed an odd-looking man in a crumpled shirt sitting across from them in the deepest corner of the restaurant writing into his spotty jotter and looking over the biggest pair of deep-rimmed glasses. "He looked like the ugliest accountant with a dead squirrel on his head!" Danning stated. She later recalled that the same guy would turn up to every meal she and Lee had.

Additional issues came in the form of SFX, as the studio seemed reluctant to provide full-body werewolf suits. Instead of Mora getting the werewolf costumes he repeatedly asked for, he got monkey outfits sent direct from California. The crates arrived stamped 'Twentieth Century Fox / *Planet of the Apes*'.

"He looked like the ugliest accountant with a dead squirrel on his head!"

Philippe Mora called the studio direct and spoke with producer John Daly, questioning the studio's strange choice of suit for a werewolf movie, but the response was, "Hey, deal with it. We can't send anything else."

Mora did deal with it, and he recreated the werewolf mythology as we know it forever. Instead of the generic scenario from man to wolf used in both books and movies up to that point in history, *Howling II* added a slice of Darwin's Theory of Evolution, but with a twist. Man had to become a monkey before he became a wolf. This unique take on lycanthropic biology is explained by Stefan (Christopher Lee) in a close-up shot in the finished film.

The next problematic issue to overcome on set was the fact the film demanded Sybil Danning (Stirba) in fully-fledged werewolf gear. To get around these technical issues, Danning, Marsha A. Hunt (*Dracula A.D. 1972*) and Judd Omen (*C.H.U.D II*) had hair glued all over their bodies, which took a total of 8 hours each in the make-up chair. During the scenes they had to refrain from touching each other as the hair would come off in their hands and more hair would have to be glued. The sex scene results in all three having sex without actually touching each other! If that wasn't punishment enough for the actors, removing the hair was – the spirit gum left the cast stinging and burned, resulting in Danning having to wear sunglasses in many of her scenes due to an allergic reaction.

During Omen's hair application Steve Johnson had to apply extra hair to Omen's genitalia to avoid the scenes receiving the dreaded R rating, towards which the film was already heading. Johnson's application was very up-close and personal, and after manhandling Omen for 30 long minutes Omen became aroused. To avoid further embarrassment Omen burst into opera to lighten the atmosphere.

The scenes hit the mark. The film was in the can and was about to become groundbreaking cinema, combining bestiality, lycanthropy, threesomes, lesbianism and interracial sex not seen in major motion pictures until *Howling II*.

The film industry has always had hang-ups about sex, so it wasn't a surprise when they were slightly concerned about the film's content when the editing process kicked off. It had pushed boundaries a little too far in a number of people's minds. Danning was upset by the fact her breasts were flashed repeatedly during the credits. Christopher Lee gagged on his latte, along with the rest of Hollywood, when he saw the finished cut of the movie, deeming the film to be nothing more than exploitative cinema, vulgar and in very bad taste.

Right until his death Lee avoided talking about the movie, refusing to acknowledge it. During one of his many one-day promotional appearances at the movie and comic showcase, London MCM Expo, his

manager stressed to all the press, "Only ask him about the album, OK?"

With the editing process complete Hemdale Films released the film theatrically in France and England in 1985, before the theatrical release in the United States in January 1986, running for 91 minutes.

The film failed to garner as much attention or commercial success as the original, so the marketing campaign in the USA dramatically changed its approach, with new poster art and a new tagline, which read, "The rocking, shocking new wave of horror!"

Critically and financially the film was a bomb. It was notably billed as a laughable exercise in horror-porn tomfoolery. Later it acquired a cult following on VHS, released by HBO / Cannon Home Video and Home Video, partly because of the presence of cult actors Sybil Danning, Reb Brown and Christopher Lee. The re-edited VHS release ran for 81 minutes and included a highlight reel wherein Danning's big, blouse-busting moment was extended and repeated an amazing seventeen times, in perfect sync with the pulsating New Wave theme song!

The TV version runs for 91 minutes. It includes a new scene before the end credits plus a brand new end credit sequence in order to replace the topless shots of Sybil Danning in the original's R-rated sequence. The TV end credits also include music, whereas the theatrical version is silent.

MGM Home Entertainment had commercial re-release of the DVD for *Your Sister Is a Werewolf* in 2005, and they released it again in 2010 as part of a two-disc set that included both 1985's *Your Sister Is a Werewolf* and 1981's *The Howling*.

But it wasn't until 2006 that the film received the Arrow special treatment, releasing the film in a dual format (High Definition

Blu-ray (1080p) and Standard Definition DVD presentations) with brand new cover art, additionally restoring the lost alternative opening and alternative ending in its bonus features.

No matter what negatives can be said about the movie's unusual style and outrageously camp direction, Philippe Mora has crafted a cult cinematic experience that is more talked about than its predecessor and that is a testament to the man behind the vision! Long live *Howling II*... ■

GARY BRANDNER ON HOWLING II

"I agreed for the same reason professional writers agree to anything – money.

"And, sure, there was a pride of authorship involved. My first draft was lovingly true to the book. At the original story meeting they said, 'Gary, this is great, but the producer would like a part for his friend Fernando Rey.'

"I dutifully went home and wrote in the veteran actor. In the next meeting I was told 'Wonderful, Gary, but the money is coming from Spaniards, and they'd like the story to take place in Spain. And, oh yes, Fernando Rey is out.'

"Okay, I bundled up my plot and my people and moved everything to Spain. Then, here we go again, 'Perfect, Gary, but the Spanish money dropped out and we're shooting on the cheap in Yugoslavia.'

"Here I had to bail out since I had a book contract with a deadline approaching. They hired another writer who is responsible for what you see on the screen. I retained co-screenwriter credits, which brings in a few dollars twice a year.

"A friend once said to James M. Cain, 'Jimmy, how can you let the movie people do that to your books?' Cain replied, 'Nobody's done anything to my books. They're all right up there on the shelf.' I couldn't do better than that."

2.

The Philippe Mora interview

By the end of 1981 *The Howling* was one of the top-grossing horror films of that year representing a new movement in cutting-edge SFX. In the wake of *An American Werewolf in London*, *The Howling* tapped into the collective fears of its audience in a way few independent Hollywood films had ever done, without following any of the well-established Hammer Horror film rules.

Four years later the industry was making horror movies faster, cheaper and gorier as audiences consumed *Day of the Dead*, *Fright Night*, *Return of the Living Dead* and *A Nightmare on Elm Street 2: Freddy's Revenge*, each pushing FX boundaries further, all competing for the same ticket-buying public, each aiming for the strongest box office opening weekend.

Then, on August 28, 1985, Hemdale Film Corporation unleashed the shocking new wave of horror – *Howling II* – so shocking that Christopher Lee later apologized to director Joe Dante for being a part of the film, so shocking that the film has gone on to be talked about more than its predecessor and continues to please festival crowds around the globe.

www.werewolves.com said of Philippe Mora's foreword to this book, "His introduction should be about ten pages long, and should consist of nothing more than Mora stating, 'I'm sorry!' over and over."

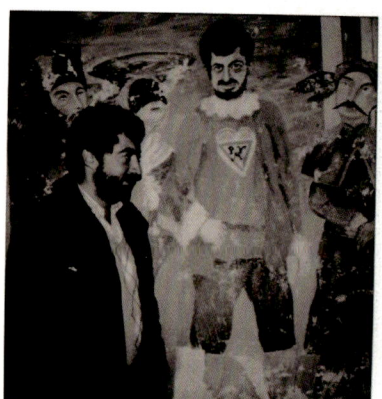

While one werewolf fan's opinion is as good as another's let me remind you that Mora went in with eyes wide open, never intending to compete with Joe Dante's celluloid gem!

He also gave fans the legendary blouse-busting visuals by Sybil Danning that still sets tongues wagging today. And without *Howling II* Mora would never have been able to give movie buffs the on-screen magic in all its hairy proportions between Sybil Danning, Marsha A. Hunt and Judd Omen.

Here's to the memories!

PHILIPPE MORA

ON THE ATTRACTION OF DIRECTING *THE HOWLING II*:

Various factors influenced me over the years regarding how I ended up directing different films. I never wanted to be typecast so I have an eclectic resume. I don't think I've ever revealed this before but I never saw Joe's movie before I made my *Howlings*. I felt that doing a sequel was a no-win situation, because if you copied the original you got no points as a director, and if you made a different film you got catcalls from the fans of the original! However, I needed a job, and the producers offered me this because I had made *The Beast Within*. So I opted to make a different film entirely and not see the original, and ditto with *Howling III*. This theory resulted in the only series in film history that I know of where each film is basically unrelated to the last. I have since seen the

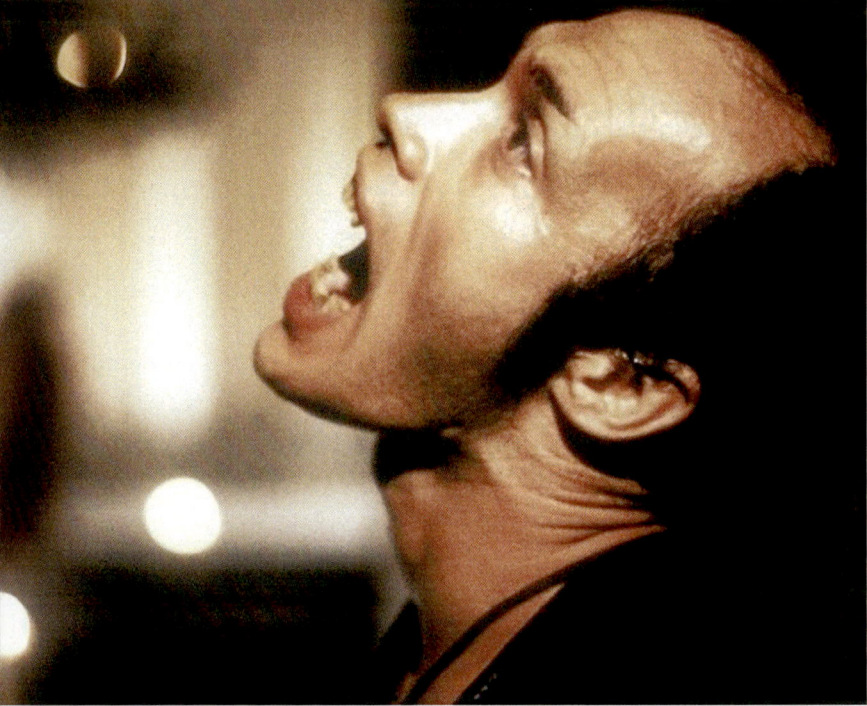

> "I asked him what "Shut Up!" in Czech was early on, to demonstrate to him what he might have to say. He said it was "CLIT!" or it sounded like that to me. This caused some confusion with the English component of the crew when I yelled it out."

original *Howling* and enjoyed it.

ON GARY BRANDNER'S THOUGHTS ON MORA'S ENTRIES:

Gary became a very good friend of mine and we planned to make another werewolf film together about a young werewolf called Marcus. We also planned another film together with Sybil about werewolf hunters. He was a charming man, and greatly missed. I don't know the details of his relations with the producers because when I came on he was already not hands-on involved. He gladly made an arrangement with me regarding *Howling III* and he thought it was a total hoot. I once asked him why people turn into werewolves. He said, "There is no reason and that is the horror of it!" Later I read that Curt Siodmak, the author of the original wolfman movie (1941), felt that, as a Jewish man on the run from Nazis, the transformation of man into monster was a metaphor for the Nazis' irrational hatred of Jews. This is why the wolfman was a sympathetic character – he had done nothing wrong and was being hunted down. I took this a little further with *Howling III*, the first openly pro-werewolf movie. I say that with a big smile because the New York Times in a very favourable review by Vincent Canby published:

> "IF you see only one werewolf movie this year, you might as well make it Howling III, Philippe Mora's not-altogether-straight-faced howler on behalf of lycanthropes' liberation. Among other things, the Australian-made movie suggests there's nothing inherently evil about being a werewolf that a little human understanding wouldn't cure. Mr. Mora and his associates are blunt about it: this anti-werewolf hysteria must stop. In the meantime, they're free to exploit it with a good deal of earnest levity."

WORKING BEHIND THE IRON CURTAIN:

The experience was not so much bizarre as incredible since it was one of the first films shot behind the Iron Curtain in Prague along with *Amadeus* and *Yentl*.

A werewolf film became a political act by default. I never felt in danger but I certainly knew I was being closely watched. We were not allowed cell phones, photocopiers or the usual tools. Instead of cell phones I was given six guys on bicycles to run messages from the set to the studio. It was a bit like working in WW1 but it worked fine once I got used to it.

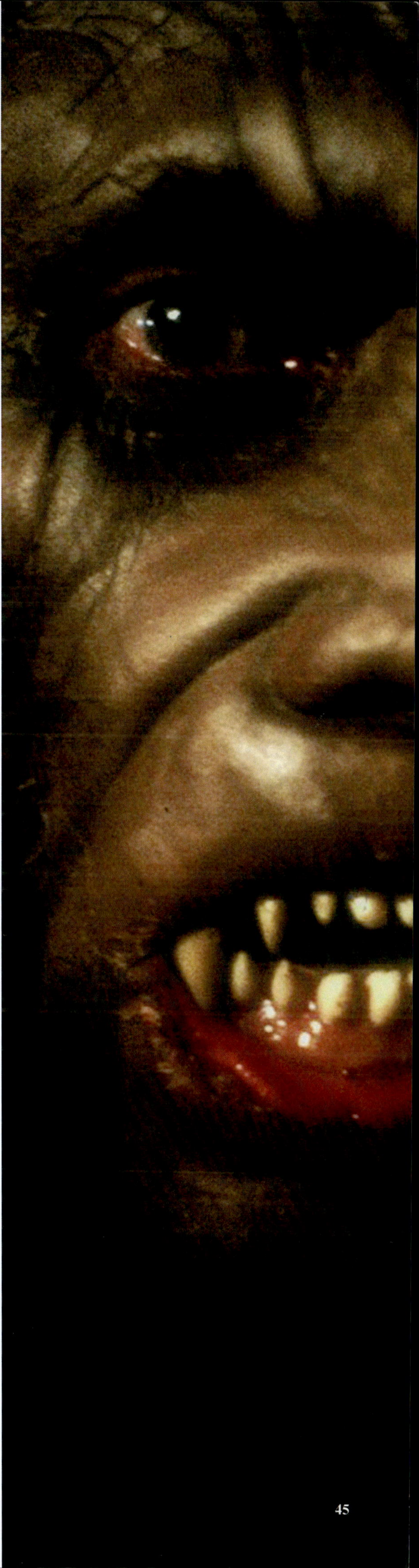

Yes, police and soldiers surrounded the studio when I shot the nightclub punk scene, and I had to speak to a Russian General and explain what I was doing. They were concerned about the size of the punk crowd we had pulled together – they had no idea what punk was or that there were so many in Prague.

This was in the Cold War, behind the Iron Curtain, and they were alarmed. They let me complete the scene quickly but then all extras had to leave three at a time in intervals of ten minutes. The manic aspect was that this was a real punk scene and they had never been allowed before to get together. It gave the scene a really electric feel.

When I got back to the hotel many young people had congregated at the front entrance and cheered me as I entered. I had no idea this would turn into a political act. It's still remembered and talked about in Prague. Who knew that *Howling II* would strike a blow for freedom?

ON SHOOTING IN PRAGUE'S CRIME SCENE MORGUE:
What went through my mind was to get out pronto!

Even though it was refrigerated the smell was demonically revolting.

I took one photo before I started gagging and left.

One associate starting screaming, running down the street trying to get an eyelid off his shoe.

ON TONY CECH BEING A KGB IN-PLANT AND COMMUNICATING WITH THE CZECH FILM CREW:

I really don't know, he didn't seem to have much experience at being an AD, but he did by the end! I asked him what "Shut Up!" in Czech was early on, to demonstrate to him what he might have to say. He said it was "CLIT!" or it sounded like that to me. This caused some confusion with the English component of the crew when I yelled it out.

THE SHOOTING FRAME:
I think it was shot in six weeks. Maybe less. With an additional shoot in LA when I got back of werewolf heads so that we were not all *Planet of the Apes*.

WORKING IN THE BARRANDOV STUDIOS:
Barrandov was pretty spectacular because it was built by Goebbels in WW2 so they could keep shooting while Berlin was bombed. We actually did not shoot there but mainly on locations – castles and so on.

ON WORKING WITH CHRISTOPHER LEE AND LEE DISASSOCIATING HIMSELF FROM THE PROJECT:
He was great to work with. I had already worked with him on *The Return Of Captain Invincible* so we had a rapport. It was bloody freezing, very low budget and also strange, even creepy behind the Iron Curtain, so it was difficult. But it added to the bizarre

atmosphere of the film.

Christopher was brilliant in the film and had no problem sending himself up, for example, wearing the sunglasses in the night club I asked him to wear.

In fact he came up with a wonderful solution to a big production problem: he overheard me in a phone conversation telling the producer, John Daly, that everyone in the world knew that *The Howling* was about werewolves, so why in the hell had he just sent me the monkey suits from *Planet of the Apes* (all the way from Los Angeles to Prague)?

Daly: "You are talented, so you figure it out!"

Mora: "This has nothing to do with talent, there are monkeys and there are wolves."

Daly then hung up on me. Christopher, rather alarmed, then said to me, " I have an idea – tomorrow film me explaining that before man turns into wolf, he goes through a monkey phase. MAN, MONKEY, WOLF! GET IT!"

I told Christopher he was brilliant and we would do exactly that. Which I did. When the film came out reviews were nasty except some said that for the first time in cinema history it is explained that before man turns into wolf he goes through a monkey phase.

He is a great artist, actor and person and that is all I can say. I'm sure he will eventually come around.

ON THE SFX AND THE TIME IT TOOK TO SHOOT THEM:

Some of the effects were great, others not.

Some of the cheesy light animation effects were added in my absence by the producers

Every scene was shot quickly in a matter of hours. They had to be.

I like the exploding little person's head because it reminds me of a Francis Bacon painting.

ON *THE HOWLING II*'S CULT VISUALS AND THE SYBIL DANNING BLOUSE-BUSTING VISUAL:

I wanted a montage of some key moments for the end credits cut to the great "pulsating" score. I found since I made *Brother Can You Spare A Dime* that editing to the beats of musical pieces could be very effective. Obviously Sybil's reveal was a great moment and I originally repeated it four or five times. I flew to Australia to start shooting *Death of a Soldier*, where the producer John Daly called me and said words to the effect; "That Sybil repeat thing you did was hilarious, what if we keep repeating it?" I replied, Go for it!"

There is a backstory to the shot. Before we started filming, Sybil asked me into her dressing room and said, "I want to show you my breasts because one is lower than the other, and they must be filmed from a certain angle so they look balanced." She revealed her breasts and said, "See what I mean, you must film them from this angle.." and she turned a bit. I said, "Yes, I see what you mean."

When I told John to go for it, I didn't mean 17 times. Maybe 10 would have done it. But when I saw it, well, it is so over-the-top and obviously funny I loved it.

SYBIL DANNING'S REACTION TO HER PULSATING BREAST PERFORMANCE:

Sybil was initially upset about it but after decades of fans saying how great she looked, she has come around. As have millions of viewers. I had no idea it would become iconic but I can make the observation that Hollywood is bizarrely paranoid about sex. Violence is OK, but God forbid you underline anything to do with SEX. So many in Hollywood, and this perhaps affected my dear friend Christopher Lee, gagged on their Lattes when they saw *Howling II*.

It's also hilarious to note that Hollywood, the Rome of vulgarity, cultural illiteracy, well-meaning but moronic kitsch and ghastly violence, thought that *Howling II* was in bad taste. Now, that is hilarious. Christopher is old school in a great way, and simply fantastic I must add, singing *Name Your Poison* in my film *The Return of Captain Invincible*.

THE HOWLING II'S HAIRY THREE-WAY ACTION:

That scene is truly surrealistic and in fact groundbreaking since it combines bestiality, lycanthropy, threesomes, lesbianism, interracial sex and something else but I've forgotten. LOL. What adds to the stylization or unreal nature of that scene is that I had to keep adding hair to Sybil as she turned into a werewolf during sexual relations. However, every time Marsha or Judd grabbed Sybil her hair would come off in their hands. So I directed them to have sexual relations without actually touching her. This resulted in such a weird ballet that I thought it was appropriate for a bizarre film and felt that Bunuel, Tod Browning and a few others were all winking at me from Heaven.

It's a highly sex-charged movie if I'm honest, hahaha.

ON THE CONFUSING 1985 THEATRICAL ADVERTISING CAMPAIGN:

Yes definitely confusing but not unusual to have different campaigns. I always like Japanese graphics. I thought the *Stirba Bitch UK* campaign humorless – it came out of nowhere.

ON THE EXPERIENCE HE GAINED FROM MAKING *THE HOWLING II* AND WHAT HE WOULD HAVE DONE DIFFERENTLY:

I knew going in this was going to be tough. But the kick for me really was the adventure of going behind the Iron Curtain. The making of the film was a lifetime experience and I will eventually make a film based on that experience called *I Was A Communist Werewolf*.

The only thing different was that I should have shot it in anamorphic 3D. ∎

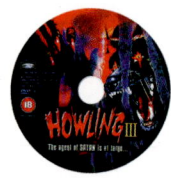

RELEASED
(USA, May 15, 1987)

DIRECTOR
Philippe Mora

WRITING CREDITS
Gary Brandner
(*The Howling I, II & III*)

STORY
Philippe Mora

SCREENPLAY
Philippe Mora

CINEMATOGRAPHER
Louis Irving

COMPOSER
Allan Zavod

CAST
Barry Otto
(Harry Beckmeyer)
Imogen Annesley
(Jerboa),
Max Fairchild
(Thylo),
Lee Biolos
(Donny Martin),
Barry Humphries
(Dame Edna)

PRODUCTION COMPANY
Embassy Pictures

EDITOR
Lee Smith

SPECIAL EFFECTS
Bob McCarron,
Nik Dorning,
Belinda Villani

RUNNING TIME
94 min

Howling III: The Marsupials

Just When You Thought It Was Safe To Go Down Under...

SYNOPSIS

It started with *The Howling*, one of the most successful horror films of the eighties, then followed the equally gruesome *Howling II*. Now there is a brand new breed of terror... *Howling III: The Marsupials*.

A tongue-in-cheek satirical thrashing of horror movies of recent years – with a new setting: Australia. When a pregnant bush girl runs away from her tribe to the city it is discovered she is part marsupial and her tribe is a pack of werewolves. Meanwhile a visiting Russian ballerina transforms into a werewolf during rehearsals. A crew filming a low budget werewolf movie is looking for a leading lady and finds Jerboa, the girl who has fled her tribe. She's been followed by her werewolf sisters, dressed as nuns, and when it seems the city is being plagued by werewolves the military is called in.

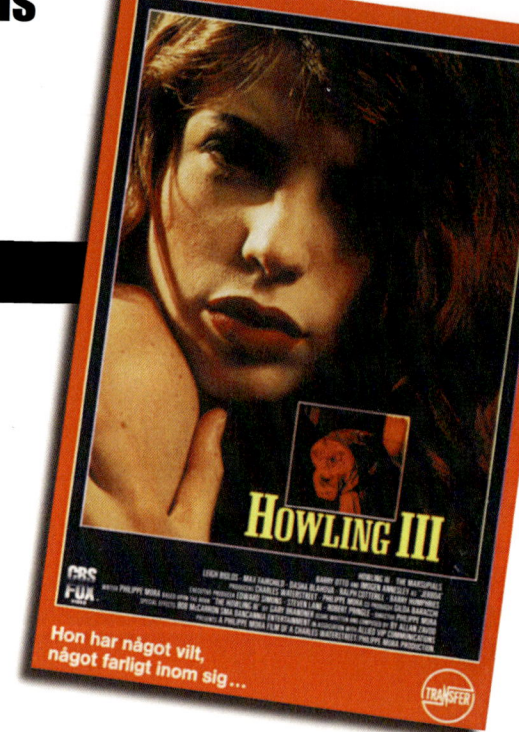

With more scares than *The Howling* and more laughs than *Teen Wolf*, *Howling III* is something different in an evening's entertainment.

The *Howling* series' continual error has always been in each film's marketing strategy and its follow up campaign. The studios behind the films never seem to know what to do with the film once it's on the distributor's shelf or who the film's target audience is in some cases (*Howling II*).

This was also a flaw in the case of Kevin Williamson and Wes Craven's collaborative effort *Cursed* (2005), a film that crashed and burned at the box office and was simultaneously panned by critics, partly due to the marketing campaign that heavily focused on the yesteryear Shannon Elizabeth (*American Pie*), who hadn't done anything notable since 2001.

Cursed was meant to reinvent the werewolf genre. Williamson's original script combined black comedy and a whodunit mystery with FX by Rick Baker (*Wolf*), which promised to be as groundbreaking as was his work within the werewolf genre in 1981. *Cursed* was also set up in such a way it was going to satirise the clichés of that sub-genre decade, popularised in such films as *Wolfen*, *An American Werewolf In London* and *The Howling*.

Cursed's attempt to subvert the genre it sat alongside failed and buried any future chance of a studio attempting to release a werewolf movie theatrically for a while. But before Wes Craven's tongue-in-cheek *Cursed* there was Philippe Mora's *Howling III: The Marsupials*, a movie that had just as much black humour and was a send-up of the Hollywood werewolf film factory clichés. It was a standalone movie, so disconnected from its very own advertising campaign it struggled to convey on the box what it actually was.

Howling III: The Marsupials still to this day makes die-hard werewolf fans' blood boil.

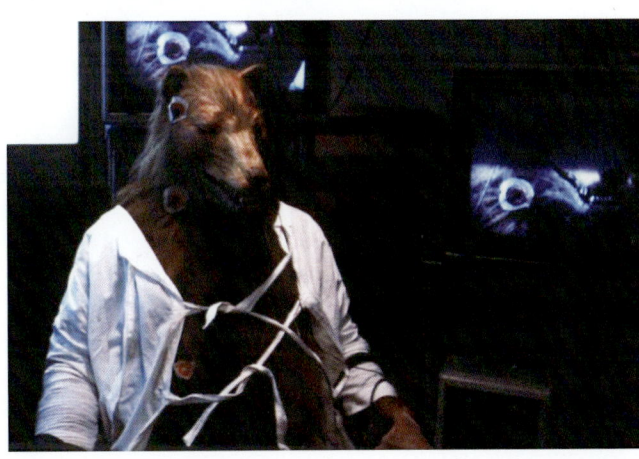

When *The Complete History of The Howling* announced via Twitter that Philippe Mora was to pen the book's foreword there was an outrage in werewolf cyber space. www.werewolves.com raged and ranted, "*The Complete History of The Howling* is written by Bryn Curt James Hammond and will feature an introduction by Philippe Mora, who directed Howling 2 and Howling 3. (This introduction should be about ten pages long, and should consist of nothing more than Mora stating "I'm sorry!" over and over. And the guy should have to write it by hand while sitting naked in a meat locker and being spritzed with freezing water. Yes, Howling 3 is THAT abysmally bad. Mora should be exposed to SAW-esque tortures for committing such a transgression.)"

Philippe Mora's (*The Beast Within*) send-up of the sub-genre was not intended to be an offshoot of *The Howling* or *Howling II*; *Howling III: The Marsupials* was conceived as a satire, as was the badly-executed *Cursed*, which heavily borrowed from Mora's self-funded movie. And while many horror fans missed Mora's punch-line *Howling III: The Marsupials* still managed to become a part of popular culture thanks to the likes of Matt Groening (*The Simpsons – Space Mutants V: The Land Down Under*), who was in on the joke which many missed. *Howling III: The Marsupials* additionally popped up in *Death In Brunswick* (1990), directed by John Ruane and starring Sam Neil.

The story of *Howling III: The Marsupials* begins rather modestly. Shortly after *Howling II*'s box office failure Hemdale had done with the brand and it looked unlikely that the series would ever rise again from beneath its wreckage but Mora, who had learned that speed can be constructive and fun, began plotting his Phoenix-rising-from-the-ashes soon after.

Unsatisfied by the previous film's commercial crucifixion due to bad marketing Mora believed that if he had full ownership and control over the movie the audience would get the joke the second time around. After all, back home in Australia suburban video store aisles were littered with tongue-in-cheek horror flicks, and had been for decades, and almost all of them were received better outside their native country. *Harlequin* (1980) and *The Cars That Ate Paris* (1974) were prime examples, the latter struggling to find its captive audience in Australia due to a confused ad campaign, but it found a home with New Line Cinema in 1976 and went on to become a cult classic and was turned into a musical.

Mora burned the candle at both ends throughout the writing process of *Howling III* and after the film draft was finished and ready to go he wasted no time in taking his script with his then producing partner, Charles Waterstreet (*Sons of Steel*), to potential investors. "We [Charles Waterstreet] tried to raise the money in Australia from Government funding but it was hopeless, even though I asked them what could be more culturally Australian than marsupial women?" stated Mora in his unique jovial manner.

The Australian Film Finance Corporation, which supported film and television productions within their own country, took one look at Mora's films concept and were left bewildered and concerned for their safety. Mora and Waterstreet were immediately escorted from the building.

Not being one to give up easily, Mora took his rejected script about a community of Tasmanian tiger inbred werewolves, nuns and ballerinas right to the Sydney Bank, a decision he wouldn't regret. Once the business plan was out of the way and the banker had heard Mora's grandiose path to glory with *Howling III: The Marsupials* he agreed without further hesitation to loan the double act a cool $1 million.

Howling III: The Marsupials, which went from concept to script in a matter of months, had now secured its modest budget, and while it was a third less than that of *Howling II*, Mora had a great team around him that could keep up with his speed – speed meant everything!

Casting *Howling III: The Marsupials* attracted a number of well-known entertainers. One of the actresses that turned up to the casting call became one of Hollywood's biggest earners – Nicole Kidman (*The Killing of a Sacred Deer*). Kidman read for the role of Jerboa, but Mora was looking for more of an animalistic actress. "Nicole read beautifully for the role and was very keen. She was not a big star at the time," said Mora. "She was beautiful."

Imogen Annesley (*Queen of the Damned*), who has relocated to Los Angeles but has since failed to make an impact on the industry, fitted the bill. "Imogen was everything I had in mind when I wrote the role." Annesley turned up, made a couple of animal noises, and before she knew it she had signed on the dotted line. She was in front of the camera even before the ink had dried.

Prior to *Howling III: The Marsupials* Annesley starred in *Playing Beatie Bow*, a film about a discontented teenager who travels back in time to 1873 whilst watching an old-fashioned children's game. The film, which began life as a children's book, was slammed due to Annesley appearing semi-nude in one scene while in another she wears the word 'shit' emblazoned across a T-shirt. Donald Crombie (*Flipper*), who directed, defended his choices but it didn't silence the critics.

Howling III: The Marsupials was shot in and around Sydney Harbour. Originally Mora wanted to take the film and

SCREAM QUEEN: IMOGEN ANNESLEY

Imogen Annesley's character, Jerboa, was set amidst an inbred community of half-men, half-marsupials. The marsupial, Jerboa, could take no more and upped sticks and headed to the big city to forget her past. Much like Jerboa, Annesley relocated to the big city in sun-kissed California. Before her role as Jerboa in *Howling III: The Marsupials* Annesley's most notable theatrical role was of a club-goer in *Queen of the Damned* (2002) and her presence on the small screen has also been as spacious, with minor recurring roles in *East of Everything* for just 7 episodes.

When approached to take part in *The Complete History of The Howling* to support her director, Philippe Mora, the jobbing actress stated the obvious: "It was 30 years ago!"

After a bit of persuading she asked to take a look at the questions. After reading over them she replied nonchalantly, "Those questions are kind of more like things you would have answered then." It's a retrospective book, "Duh" – Cher (*Clueless*, 1995).

Annesley deliberately waited to reply until after the specified deadline, then added, "And seems I

missed the date anyway just getting this!"

Ignoring her previous DM I asked the actress if she had any funny stories she would like to share for the book and she followed up with her final message, "There are funny stories that Philip prob told, And yes it continues to be in my life as its in not quite Hollywood etc and people bring it up a lot".

Take from that what you will, readers.

---

shoot it in the Blue Mountains and Alice Springs, but budget restrictions killed those plans. Previously he had shot in the bush when making *Mad Dog Morgan* (Dennis Hopper), so he was fully prepared for what obstacles the bush would throw his way.

The special effects team was managed by Bob McCarron, whose work has included *The Matrix* (1999), *Dead Alive* (1992) and *Mad Max 2: The Road Warrior* (1981). Creating the SFX was a challenge as there were several different designs to create and Mora's unique style of slapstick gore pushed the envelope. "I was more into giving the audience some frights as well as the obvious (to me) humour," Mora stated. "Bob McCarron is a great FX artist" and "Bravo to him!"

Mora gave McCarron (*Queen of the Damned*) the green light to go overboard with the FX and not to give a damn. "The odder the better, just run with it." So the rest, as they say, was history, and that's just what McCarron did.

Howling III: The Marsupials was edited under Mora's watchful eye by Oscar winner Lee Smith (*X-Men: Dark Phoenix*). Almost everything from the script that made it into the can ended up in the final edit.

Mora's film mixed a political landscape with the Hollywood system and for added measure a romantic backdrop. The film also had a very real message that was very close to Mora's heart – anti-hunting. "I am against hunting," he stressed. "People simply don't care. The killing of the Thylacine to extinction is a tragedy."

The Marsupials highlights the Thylacine tragedy throughout the film, which is similar in tone to Gary Brandner's *The Howling III: Echoes*. *Echoes* shines a more sympathetic light on its werewolf (Malcolm), turning the tables on the humans who are now the hunters.

Howling III: The Marsupials was the final *Howling* movie, to date, to go theatrical. Mora's elevated laughs and tongue-in-cheek satire was

confusing to most, leaving its audience much like the Australian Film Finance Corporation – bewildered. "Sometimes it takes time to be understood, although how anyone could take *Howling III* as 'straight' is still beyond me," stated Mora. But the most damaging aspect for *Howling III: The Marsupials* was the film's overseas advertising campaigns.

Market agencies hired by distributors to promote movies are never the most reliable creatures. When observing them in their own habitat these fresh-out-of-high-school wannabe hot shots spend most of their time discussing campaigns in their local wine bars before hitting the phones hard to their preferred media outlets and not what suits their client's needs.

The marketing campaign for *Howling III: The Marsupials* focused predominantly on the film's horror and psyched its audience into a frenzy with the belief they were getting a taut torrent of violence, the

definitive werewolf shocker so far, forgetting that, while it did have a horror theme running throughout, it was much more National Lampoon than the Universal Monsters. The UK's Vista Home Video's trailer campaign didn't fare any better by sampling the score from *A Nightmare on Elm Street*, with the voiceover stressing to the viewer, "They are here, they are real, and they are born of the devil!" before the blood-red title appears on the screen.

Vista Home Video's approach in the USA was just as in-your-face. Their trailer, which was released early in October, 1987 following *Howling III: The Marsupials* purchase after its marketplace screening at Cannes in May, 1987, opens with the torture of a werewolf before cutting to Max Fairchild (Thyo) strapped to a chair asking what the device is that's pointing at him. When informed it is a camera he begins to pose like a scene from TLC's *Honey Boo Boo*. The trailer features several scenes from the movie, interspersed with letters intercepting onto its black screen foreground until its intertitle *The Howling III: The Marsupials* is complete, with the theme tune *Wipe Your Tears Away* by Vitamin Z playing in the background. The campaign, while clever, still whitewashed the film's actual tone, which left the film vulnerable to criticism and open to misunderstanding.

Many years later similar elements and themes would be made popular in Wes Craven's *Scream* (1996), written by Kevin Williamson (*Dawson's Creek*). Even though Williamson has never openly stated that *Howling III: The Marsupials* influenced his tone of work, there are far too many themes running throughout *Scream III* and *Cursed* to completely ignore and put down to coincidence.

And the legend himself, Craven (August 1939 - 30 August 2015), was no stranger to regurgitating formulas from his own films. *Scream 2* (1997) lifts a segment directly from his earlier movie *The Hills have Eyes 2* (1984), which critics missed when praising *Scream 2* for its originality.

Whether such elements were or weren't borrowed Mora has proved himself both as a competent writer and a unique director. *Mad Dog Morgan*, while poorly received in his home country, went on to sell well in units around the world, even becoming a Tromasterpiece. *The Beast Within*, a loose adaptation of Edward Levy's 1981 novel of the same name, carved out a respectable opening weekend at the box office in 1982 and *Howling III: The Marsupials* rented out in hordes, sending it right up the rating charts. "Satire and parody are very difficult because you rely on the intelligence of the audience," Mora said with a smile and a glint in his eye, "which is uncontrollable."

Howling III: The Marsupials was *The Howling*'s *Jaws 3, People 0* (defunct *Jaws III* project) and has continued to gain a following on TV in the USA. "Yes, it continues to be in my life," Annesley stated, adding, "as it's in *Not Quite Hollywood* etc. and people bring it up a lot." ■

3.

The Philippe Mora interview

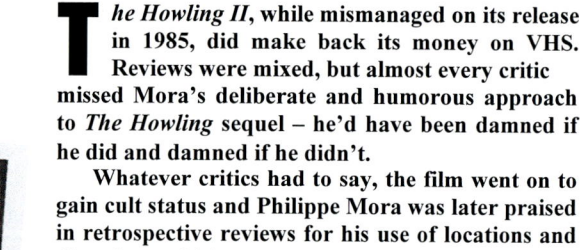

The *Howling II*, while mismanaged on its release in 1985, did make back its money on VHS. Reviews were mixed, but almost every critic missed Mora's deliberate and humorous approach to *The Howling* sequel – he'd have been damned if he did and damned if he didn't.

Whatever critics had to say, the film went on to gain cult status and Philippe Mora was later praised in retrospective reviews for his use of locations and direction, which would go on to feature in later movies within the franchise.

The iconic director (*The Beast Within*), who always had his left eyebrow raised and his tongue firmly pressed against his right cheek, never shied away from a challenge and pressed ahead with *Howling III: The Marsupials*.

His unique talent crafted a werewolf satire with slapstick horror, or "goromedy" as Mora puts it, a sub-horror genre that would later become a thing in 1996 with the release of Wes Craven's *Scream*.

Howling III: The Marsupials may have made foes of die-hard werewolf fans and even some of its stars but Mora once again left his undeniably quirky and entertaining stamp on the horror genre in a year where *Howling III: The Marsupials* should have been buried without a trace when going head to head with the likes of *Evil Dead II*, *The Lost Boys* and *Nightmare on Elm Street III: Dream Warriors*.

Yet thirty years on bloggers and YouTube reviewers continue to take on Mora's werewolf spoof with enthusiasm; still with varied degrees of praise, but importantly people are still talking!

In his own words Philippe Mora returns to his old hunting ground for a retrospective look at the *Howling III: The Marsupials* – 30 years on!

PHILIPPE MORA

FROM *HOWLING II* TO *III*, AND WHY RETURN:
I really wanted to do another *Howling* and send up the genre but with a twist: marsupial werewolves. I always loved the newsreel of the reel *Thylacine*, the last film of the extinct animal. An incredible creature, so that was my starting point.

ON HOW *HOWLING III* CAME TOGETHER:
It was totally independent so I pitched it to a bank in Sydney with my then producing partner Charles Waterstreet and they gave us the money immediately: $1 million.

This was after the then Australian Film Finance Corporation rejected it because it was a horror film and Australian women had pouches in it. There was a certain lack of humour there for sure.

I wrote the script in Sydney fairly quickly and we raised the budget quickly because *Howling II* had made a lot of money. I think *Howling III* was a third or less of the budget of *Howling II* so it was a good bet. I had a great Aussie crew, many of whom I had worked with before, so I knew I could deliver.

HOWLING III VS SCREAM, THE EVALUATION:
I've never seen the *Scream* movies. The original *Howling III* script and the finished film are pretty much the same: the irony and

sendup were there from day one. After all, the werewolves are marsupial. Anyone who does not think marsupial werewolves are an amusing concept should not bother seeing the film. On the other hand an executive producer asked me before I filmed it, "Are you sure this is a horror film?" I answered, "Have you ever seen a marsupial birth – the foetus basically crawls up from the vagina into the pouch." He said, "You're right, that's gross. Go for it."

ON PARODYING THE GENRE:
I always found it intriguing that Lon Chaney was so sympathetic in the original *Wolfman* (1941). It turns out that according to Curt Siodmak, the writer, the wolfman was a metaphor for Jews on the run from irrational hatred in Nazi Germany. I took this further with *Howling III* and it was noted by the *New York Times* in a very favourable review that this was a pro-werewolf film. I got a huge kick out of that. In retrospect my script was pretty wild but I knew at this budget it was safe to go haywire with the story.

ON NICOLE KIDMAN'S AUDITION FOR JEROBA AND WHY IMOGEN ANNESLEY BAGGED THE ROLE:
Nicole read beautifully for the role and was very keen. She was not a big star at the time. She was beautiful, smart and would have been an excellent Jerboa. At the time I was looking for a more animalistic Jerboa and found her in Imogen. I don't like casting very much because often all the actors are tremendous and it's difficult making a decision. Imogen was everything I had in mind when I wrote the role, but I had not met Imogen.

She was simply gorgeous, sensual and charismatic when she walked into the room and blew us all away. She made some animal noises and that was that.

FROM CONCEPT TO SCRIPT:

This was fast as I recall. A matter of months. The whole thing had to be done quickly because of the modest budget, and I think the speed accounts for a freshness the film still has. It's crisp.

BARRY HUMPHRIES ON SET:
My relationship to Barry is very personal since he knew me as a kid. He was part of a bohemian and artistic circle around my family with Charles Blackman, the Percevals and the Boyds. I always thought and still do that he is a comic genius and completely unique. He is hilarious. When I introduced him to Beverly D'Angelo on set she said, "Barry, I love your work and this is an honour to work with you." He replied, dressed a Dame Edna, "Beverly, I feel the same way about you, and last night I worshipped you with my own body."

My first paying job was working for Peter Sellers so I was quite at home directing Barry.

SUB PLOTS – FAMILY DRAMA, ROMANCE, ANIMAL CRUELTY AND ENVIROMENTAL ISSUES

AND THE FILM'S REACTION:

In my script: plot, plot, plot. In fact, I am sending up the early Hollywood trend continued to this day, to have uber elaborate plots and plot twists. As a kid watching movies I turned off at romantic scenes and plot. I'm a bit smarter now, but plot is no substitute for visceral feelings and action. On the other hand Shakespeare is full of detailed exposition of plot.

Re hunting and ecology, I am personally against hunting. Global warming is a fact, so ecological issues are paramount for the future. The weird thing is how many people simply don't care. The killing of the Thylacine to extinction is a tragedy and it's amazing still for me to see the newsreel film of that extraordinary animal.

Regarding reaction to this film it has taken years to be understood by some. I believe this is because satire is very difficult for some people to understand. If you break cinematic conventions as well, some people's spark plugs simply disintegrate and they don't get what they are watching.

ON *HOWLING III*'S FILM WITHIN A FILM AND OTT SFX:

I have always been amused by a Japanese film called *Voyage to the Seventh Planet*. Since part of my brain is still in High School I still crack up when in that movie, someone says to the Captain of a spaceship, "Sir, we are approaching Uranus." Captain, "OK, take it gently."

This stupid gag inspired the film within a film and I actually somewhere have a script called *It Came From Uranus*. Incredibly an executive at Hemdale Film Corporation said the script was too "cerebral" and they wouldn't make it.

I was more into giving the audience some frights as well as the obvious (to me) humour. Bob McCarron is a great FX artist and he did all this moving skeleton gag on a miniscule budget. It was very tough with no margin for error. Bravo to him!

Anyway, I was able to let loose with the mini film in *Howling III*. I told Bob McCarron, the FX maven, to go totally overboard with the designs. The funny thing is it seems you can't really go overboard enough in horror, but this really worked for me. I also told Louis Irving to really screw up the lighting, mix temperatures and so on. The result to me looks great. It's fascinating that when you tell talented people to deliberately screw up they still come up with great stuff despite themselves! Mistakes can be good!

The film was shot very quickly and that does not give much time for contemplation. It was shot simply with a lot of deep focus and Louis Irving did a great job filming with alacrity. Outdoors is easier so a lot takes place in the sun. I also liked the idea of a horror movie in the sunlight.

HOWLING III BREAKING THE MYTHOLOGY MOULD:

> "I told Bob McCarron, the FX maven, to go totally overboard with the designs. The funny thing is it seems you can't really go overboard enough in horror, but this really worked for me."

I may have mentioned elsewhere that I always remembered that newsreel footage from an early age and it stuck in my mind and inspired this film with a healthy message. Because I had creative control I was able to film things you probably could not get past a committee. So-called "script development" kills a lot of great ideas. Evolution is a subject that fascinates me and Australia's unique fauna and flora is extraordinary. Marsupial mammals may be actually a smarter creation since if the mother dies the baby still has a chance.

STROBE LIGHTS, WEREWOLVES AND EPILEPTIC FITS:

I read that strobe lights can generate epileptic fits, so it was not a big jump for me to suggest it could cause a transformation in a werewolf. Yes I could take it further. In *Howling II* I kind of implied that sexual activity can also turn you into a werewolf. This happens in the notorious menage a.... scandal.

THE HITCHCOCK HOMAGE:

Yes Frank Thring is obviously in Hitchcockian mode. I loved that actor and relished working with him. After all, he did start the chariot race in *Ben Hur*! He had the most obscene stories and jokes to tell I have ever heard except for stories from Robert Mitchum.

DISTILLING THE MYTH OF THE GOVERNMENT FUNDING RUMOUR:

We tried to raise the money in Australia from Government funding but it was hopeless, even though I asked them what could be more culturally Australian than marsupial women?

This didn't go down well with tourism minded bureaucrats or whatever the agenda was. Finally we simply borrowed the money from a bank as a straight commercial loan based on the track record of the two previous *Howlings*. One million was pretty low so we were OK. The film was set in Australia because of the Thylacine theme.

ON *HOWLING III* POPPING UP IN POPULAR CULTURE, INCLUDING THE SIMPSONS HALLOWEEN HOMAGE:

Well, honestly it's thrilling to see the film appreciated more and more as time goes by. It seems the new generations have better humour genes, and know their horror film history.

LOCATION, LOCATION, LOCATION:
I know this is corny but I love the Opera House and Sydney Harbour Bridge locations. I always have also liked shooting in the bush since I made *Mad Dog Morgan*. If we had more money I would have done something in the Blue Mountains as well as something in Alice Springs.

HOWLING II VS *HOWLING III*:
At this point in time it's hard to separate the two films into a favourite and lesser liked. I think they are both so totally different I can't compare them – and I like that because that was the concept – the rather crazy notion of sequels that are unrelated!

HOWLING III 'S EVER-CHANGING CRITICAL OPINIONS THROUGH THE DECADES:
Well, that is really gratifying. The misunderstandings come from the fact that culturally illiterate people think satire or parody is simply incompetent "serious" film making. It's hilarious really.

I think the new generation of audiences are more savvy and tired of formulaic porridge from the studios. They immediately spot originality and unlike in previous decades they feel originality is a positive thing. Personally I always liked unusual or surreal movies starting with the anarchistic comedies of the Marx Brothers and the still startling horror masterpiece, *Freaks*.

ON IF HE HAD A TARDIS:
I would have shot it in IMAX – I have always thought it would be very funny to shoot a very low budget movie in IMAX as a gag in itself.

ON REMAKING *HOWLING II* OR *III*:
Remakes are profoundly boring to me. Why do it? If the original film is superb why remake it? It can never surpass the original and rarely improves it. In that vein I thought a great gag would be to remake *Citizen Kane* with lousy actors.

ON *HOWLING III*'S MARKET CAMPAIGN:
The original campaign was OK but emphasized shock horror without a hint of wit.

Getting the film made like this was bit of a tightrope act between humour and horror. So I didn't suggest yuks in the poster. A more sophisticated campaign may have kicked it up a notch.

HAVING HIS LAST SAY ON *HOWLING III*:
It was hard and fast to get it done and very enjoyable to see an unusual film like this get a decent theatrical release across the U.S.

The video was a hit and spawned yet more sequels. The icing on the cake was the excellent review by Vincent Canby in the New York Times, who got the joke! ■

WHAT'S HAIRY, HOT, WILD, GETS YOU SCREAMING, AND IS EVEN BETTER THE 4TH TIME AROUND?

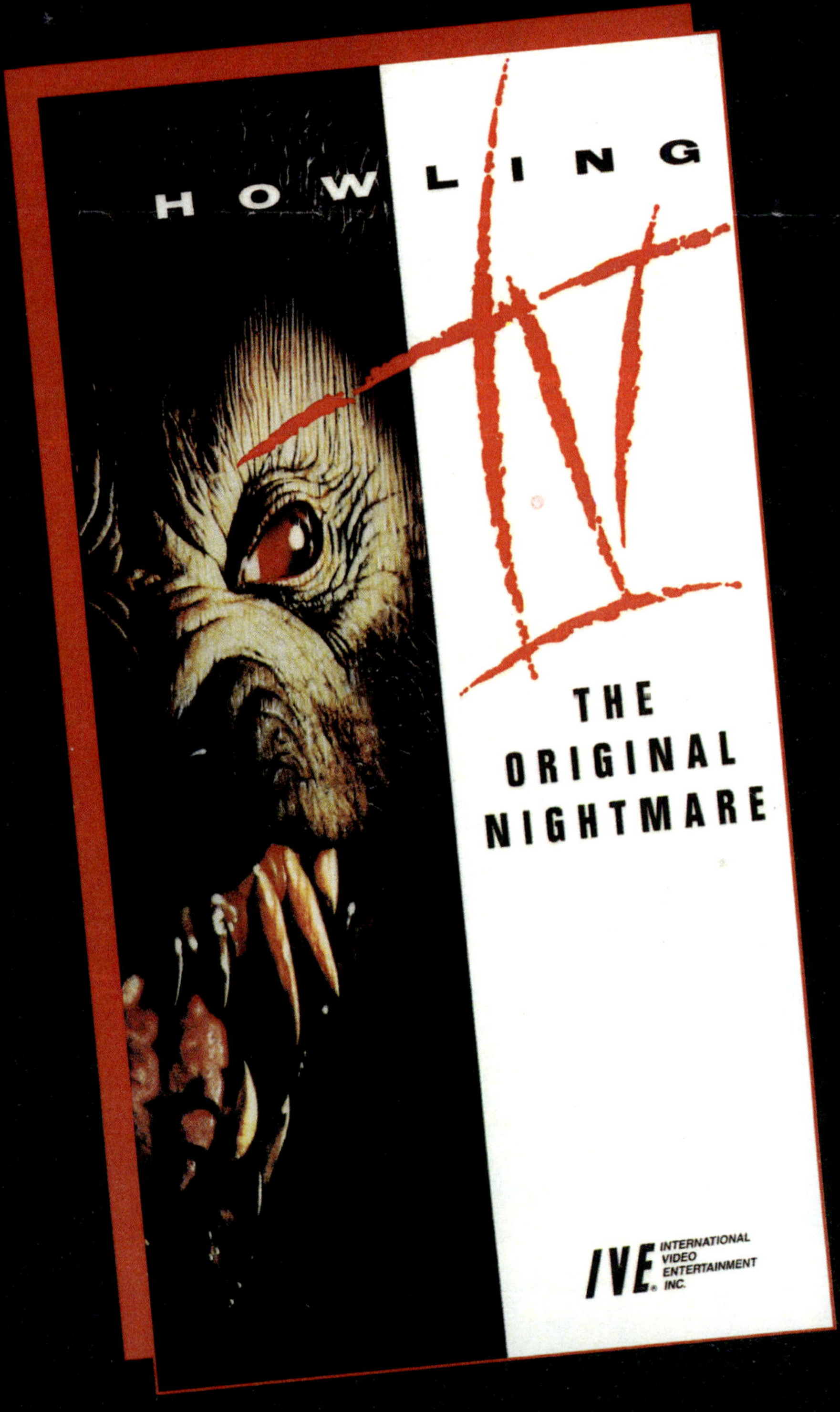

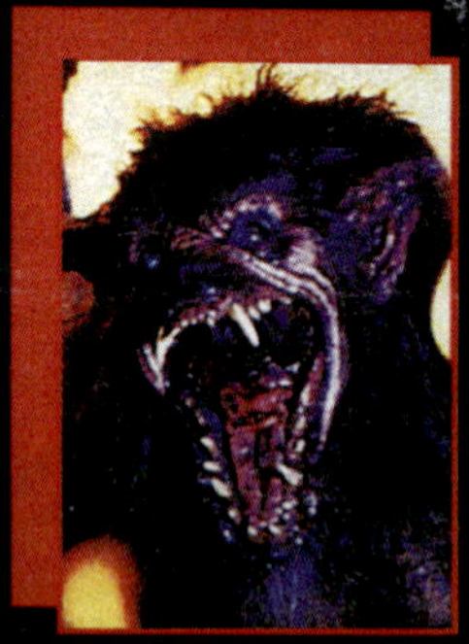

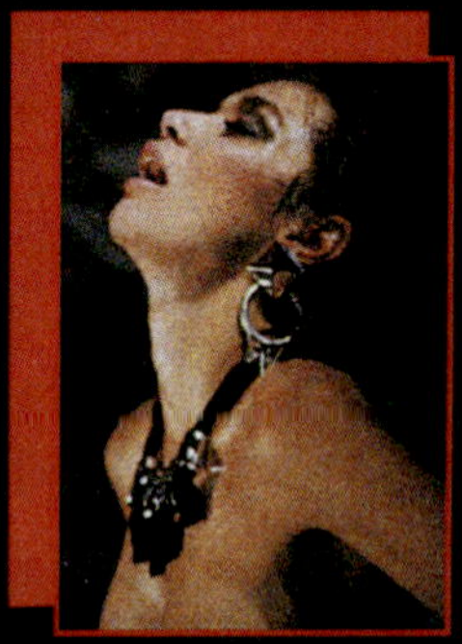

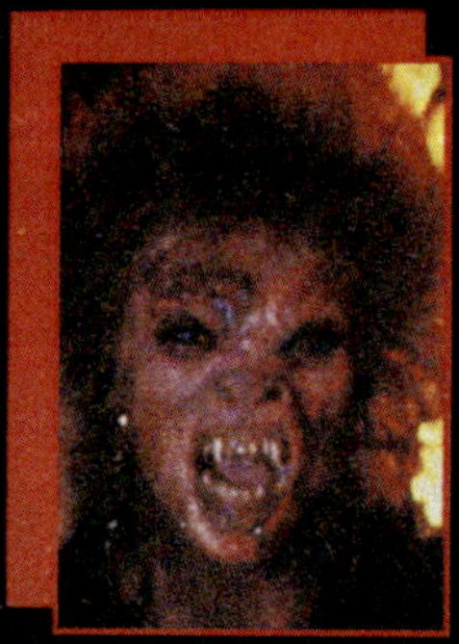

IVE INTERNATIONAL VIDEO ENTERTAINMENT INC.

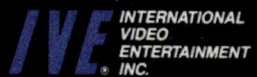

THE ULTIMATE WEREWOLF MOVIE NOW ON VIDEO!

BILL [BULL] FORSCHE

Story by **BILL FORSCHE**

I began writing my introduction to *Howling IV: The Original Nightmare* shortly after the late winter Michigan storm that greeted the 10 million residents with over 2 feet of snow, which put me way behind with lots of things. I have only just cleared a path to my postal box so I can get my mail again and begin to function.

Writing this introduction has brought back a lot of memories. *Howling IV* was a fun film to work on and it's also the movie where I acquired and embraced the name Bull Forsche for playing the werewolf because of how my name, Bill, was pronounced with the South African accent…..it sounded like Bull to me and I thought it'd make a good stage name. Additionally to changing my name this was the first time I had a passport and did some globe-trotting, and that for me made it a very interesting experience all round.

At that point in my life I rocked the 80s casual stubble, which George Michael would later adopt. It's not just coincidental; I used to work at a bar and grill in Beverly Hills and the owner let me get by with stubble as shaving a tough beard every day gave me terrible rashes, and the next thing I knew George had assumed my trade mark look and was working it all over the LA scene!

Anyhow I digress. I will return to the path that took me to South Africa. My interest in FX began as a young man after watching countless horror films. I had a gravitational pull towards the monster sub-genre and I liked science fiction films as well, and I just kind of figured that there

were film tricks that made such magic happen on screen and I wanted to be a part of it. I did a lot of studying then I started practising the craft with materials I found around the house, and one of my first projects was a papier-mâché Frankenstein head. It was fun to change my face and naturally, like every other 15-year-old, I had no patience to wait for bigger things to happen organically, so I disguised myself with a false beard, a fake ID and $15 in my back pocket and hitchhiked out of Wisconsin to Hollywood, where I became a Universal Studios tour guide to make ends meet. It was there I met make-up artist David B. Miller, who gave me insights into the business and a great deal of encouragement. His wealth of knowledge gave me the much-needed push to continue on my road to success.

As I entered 1980, the year of *Friday the 13th*, *The Shining* and *Star Wars: The Empire Strikes Back*, I returned home to Wisconsin to visit my family, which eventually led me to working with Wisconsin Bill Rebane on the horror film *The Game*. Working on the film stretched my ever-broadening horizon within the industry and once the film was complete I packed my suitcase again and headed off on my travels, this time to New York City to meet the legendary FX master Dick Smith. I had been corresponding with Smith since I was 14 and during my time spent under his wing he provided me with fatherly advice, career encouragement and guidance, which took me back to Hollywood to continue my special effects make-up and sculpting career.

It was now the late 80s, the period of big shoulders, underwear as outerwear and oversized everything, the decade of the power dresser but also of punks. The decade that gave us Pet Shop Boys, Madonna, Tina Turner and Cher and the decade of cinematic excess. It was a magical time for werewolves with that [*The Howling*] and *American Werewolf* coming out basically at the same time, both fantastic for different reasons; horror fans were having all their birthdays and Christmases at once. Rick Baker was involved in both projects. In *American*

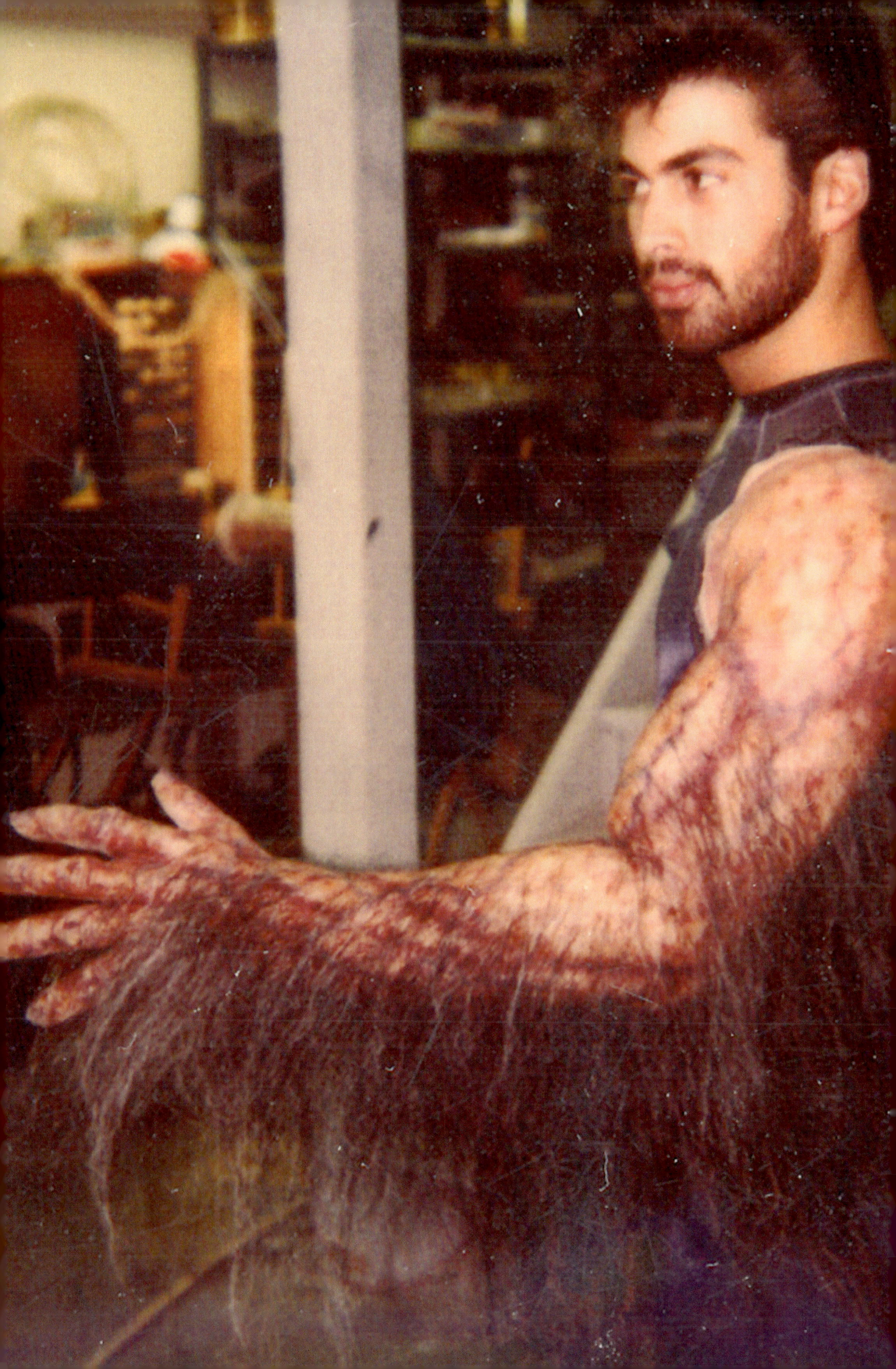

Werewolf a lot of the atmosphere was taken away intentionally because they were really showcasing that they could make the transform in real time in real lighting without hiding anything, whereas with Joe Dante's *Howling* all that atmospheric lighting looked more EC Comics in a good way. Little did I know a few years on I would also become part of *The Howling* history and lycanthrope celluloid film lore.

I was working with Steve Johnson and XFX, Inc. on a film called *Dead Heat*, directed by Mark Goldblatt, about two policemen that are brought back to life to chase down supernatural criminals when I overheard that a production company was making another *Howling* movie and they needed someone to play the fully-transformed werewolf. Admiring the original movie for its boundary-pushing, audience-stimulating FX I didn't want the role to get away, so without a second thought I volunteered to play the werewolf. I thought I would really like to do that. I was in great shape and I figured that it would be a new thing for me to do. Also I'd be able to gain an insight into what the actors get put through.

I didn't need to read the script as it was a no-brainer. What young male doesn't want to embrace his animal instincts? But looking back now, shame on me! Out of all the scripts I have in my collection that's one I have not got. I don't even think I was ever given one. But the whole situation was really run-and-gun, things happened really fast.

Once filming began I was one of the first people to fly out to South Africa accompanied by Steve Johnson. The costume was completed back at XFX, Inc. workshop. Back then studios didn't micromanage every step of the concept process so we did our thing and they left us alone, then we flew out once the final adjustments had been made to the costume. Steve and I were good friends; we are no longer good friends, but hey, this is Hollywood. Flying out together made

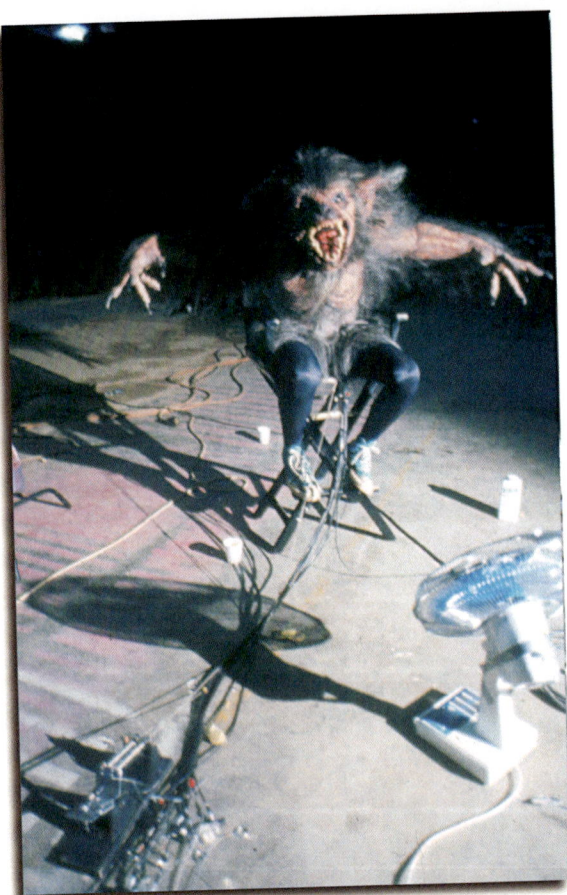

> **"I said, "Can we leave their collars on so that I have something to hold, so I can hold their faces back if anything goes wrong?" The trainer told me they go for the throat, and my face was in the throat area of the costume, so that didn't give me much confidence."**

logical sense. Prior to leaving I spoke with Dick; it was my first time flying out of the country and he gave me a pep talk and some good advice about travelling, food and so on, things you do have to be aware of when you're out of your own habitat and in a different country.

When I arrived in South Africa the first thing that hit me was I was no longer in Hollywood. I was a fish out of water and I could hear the infamous line from The Wizard of Oz, "Toto, I've a feeling we're not in Kansas any more," but I wasn't going to let fear get in the way of my experience; I was young and ready to rock 'n' roll. The jet lag on the other hand was difficult to deal with. When I arrived on the set it became apparent we didn't have good air conditioning, which normally helps keep you fresh when you're working extremely long days, and when we were shooting outside with the big lights on, oh my God, we freaked out with all the bugs. The bugs were attracted to the lights and combine that with the food that was kicking around they were having a feast.

The hardest part about filming in South Africa was that it was difficult to bring a lot of our own things from the workshop back in California. We were designated a person that we dealt with locally and he could get us a lot of the things we needed, but when you're used to having a lot of your own products readily available that is difficult. Back home we had suppliers on our doorstep but things in South Africa worked very differently. That's all part of the learning curve and I welcomed every obstacle as it kept things interesting and took my mind off the jet lag and the scary orange

drink which was like concentrated. Steve was dispirited over his substitute for Marlboro Lights, Dunhill International Lights, but what he did like about Dunhill was the wonderful packaging, which was a joke among the XFX, Inc. crew.

The first scene I worked on was with Mike Weiss, the scenes where his shoulder was bleeding after he was bitten or scratched by Lamya Derval – I can't recollect the minute details. The working hours were long, but that's normal in a low budget film anyway. It didn't seem too out of the ordinary to me but things did become a little bit of a fog, jet lag amnesia.

Anyway, we were out in the middle of nowhere and didn't have everything in the makeup kit we needed to match his chest hair – he had just a little bit of fluff around where I did the application, so I volunteered some of mine! I don't know how hygienic it was but it did the trick, it worked really well, we were on the ground running; out came the scissors and glue and the job was complete, it was all very guerrilla filmmaking at its very best, or worst, depending how you look at it.

Mike, who came fresh from *Days Of Our Lives*, had his moments. I wouldn't say he was difficult to work with but he was not a happy camper with all that he had to endure. I don't blame him, as a lot of the paint was very difficult to remove. Because of where we were we had to use the remover sparingly as we didn't have as much as we would like to have. We really didn't have the facilities to do a lot of location work. It was really, really difficult but everyone was quite nice. Romy Windsor was very kind. I remember I spent my birthday there in November and she sang the full Happy Birthday song to me. She was really wonderful to work with. ….

Filming on location had its difficulties as well but I got on very well with everyone, including Clive [Turner], who was the on-set producer, writer and drug dealer; he was the man to go to for absolutely anything. But I don't know how much of the drama between him and John Hough was true [is true], but their relationship was out of the ordinary. I don't think it was over the top, but I do remember John asserting himself on certain things, and there were times that the shots or some of the set dressings didn't come up to par, come up to speed, and it was good that some things were addressed assertively. There weren't really any big arguments when I was directly involved with the filming or the applications – but there was an underlying tension and times that, with the weather and the lack of air conditioning, it was like a pressure cooker. In the summertime everyone's hot and everyone gets a little cranky, especially when you're working late.

John Hough was interesting to work with, and I think he had a lot on his plate – it was one long juggling act for him. When I first got there he wasn't the kindest, but it's not his job to be kind. I was videoing everything; he would see me filming and he said to me, "Instead of doing that, why don't you show me some eyes that work?" I put some contacts in and then applied some burn makeup to one of the local actors and it really read well on film and it looked really good. He claimed that was an ace job and from that point it was like, "You're ok."

One of the most difficult effects to achieve was where the doctor, played by the wonderful Dennis Folbigge, has the jaw underneath his face. That was Bruce Zahlava's project. I had worked with Zahlava on *Dead Heat* prior to *Howling*. There was a fully mechanized smile mechanism that would pull back the lips and so on, but it really didn't function well, so since it wasn't working we opted to push blood into the area where the fake teeth are glued to the outside of his chin in the mouth area. The mechanization wasn't translating well so we had Steve inject blood and we had him pull away the foam, which of course looked like he was tearing his own skin apart. That actually read pretty well and was one of the ones that got applause on set from the cast and crew.

An interesting point of me playing the werewolf, there was a scene which involved me interacting with real dogs and I had to pay meticulous attention to detail when John Hough and the trainer explained what was going to happen and how it was going to happen due to their concern for my safety. The dogs used were actually prison attack dogs whose job was to return the prisoners if they ever break out of jail. And you know what, they say if the dogs bring them back living that's ok, and if they don't that's probably ok too! They were big and scary. The trainer was not a Hollywood trainer; he worked with the prison guard dogs for a living. I said, "Can we leave their collars on so that I have something to hold, so I can hold their faces back if anything goes wrong?" The trainer told me they go for the throat, and my face was in the throat area of the costume, so that didn't give me much confidence. I told John, "You know what, you need to show me what I need to do for a take, and then I'll do it!" The production company at that time didn't have a really good reputation and there was talk that some stuntmen got hurt and/or killed – I don't know if that was just hearsay or not, but it raised a lot of eyebrows and I was definitely concerned.

It was during my many flights back and forth, usually talking my way into First Class – I didn't pay for First Class but I figured I could talk my way in. This was the days when planes weren't full, which was just amazing and during one of my trips I became aware of Cannon Films' connection with my film. So while in First Class I met a beautiful young lady wearing knee high socks and she had this kind of teeny bopper outfit on. We started talking and she asked me what I was doing and I said, "Well, I'm working on this film and it's *Howling IV* and we're filming in Johannesburg." She said, "Oh, well I'm flying out to see

my friend Harry Alan Towers." I wasn't aware of his presence on set when I was filming. I think Towers was more like the godfather. But he had a very colourful reputation. *Howling IV: The Original Nightmare* was one of Towers and Avi Lerner's non-Cannon films but Cannon's reputation preceded them.

The final sequence where I filmed the fire sequence, Nick Benson and Eric Fielder built a fire rig in the parking lot of XFX, Inc. to be used in the scene. The suit was incredibly uncomfortable, the head rested on top of my head, so there was a lot of weight on my eye sockets. It made my eyes quite puffy and I looked like a prize fighter. People were pretty good to me on set and knew they had to have fans ready and keep me hydrated. When I was in the fire sequences they were still applying hair spray to me and I had to keep reminding them, "That's flammable!" It was an intense shoot, it was hot as hell and it was in the summertime!

> "The suit was incredibly uncomfortable, the head rested on top of my head, so there was a lot of weight on my eye sockets. It made my eyes quite puffy and I looked like a prize fighter."

After the film wrapped re-shoots began. I think I was there for a day or two but I was not directly involved. The final cut of the film wasn't what I envisioned; the pacing was a little slow. The acting was good but – and this is nothing to do with me portraying the werewolf – I don't think there was enough of the werewolf in the whole finished film. There really is not much of the full werewolf, and it looked really good. I wish that could be re-edited. The cut the public have available is heavily cut; we shot a hell of a lot that never made it into the finished film. A lot of the suit work wasn't in; all that work with the prison dogs just didn't make it. From what I recall the transformation seems to run long and the pacing is a little off. I'm disappointed!

The film's wrap party was held at IDOLS nightclub in Johannesburg on 96 End Street. IDOLS was a popular dance club, a legendary place and famous for going on non-stop right through to Sunday night. It was an unforgettable evening. I loaned Lamya my jacket, she additionally was wearing my leather jacket in the film and it still has the white dot on it that signified we were clear for the VIP section in the club.

I have many fond memories of *Howling IV: The Original Nightmare* and while I think the film became the studio's bastard child project and the timing wasn't right, when it came time to get it released properly it kinda lost legs. That's where you really need a little extra steam. You'll find it in the two dollar bin – always.

And sure, the transformation seems to run long and the pacing is a little off. I am sure now it would seem laborious. But I thought parts of the film were really good. It would be nice to see John's vision see the light of day, but I do not know if the studio even has his cut. It might be possible they do and it would be wonderful to know.

But until then here's to *Howling IV: The Original Nightmare*. ■

In Memory Of
Anton Rupprecht (Tony Rupprecht),
Antony Hamilton.

RELEASED
(USA, Nov 30, 1988)

DIRECTOR
John Hough,
Clive Turner

WRITING CREDITS
Gary Brandner
(*The Howling I, II & III*)

STORY
Clive Turner

SCREENPLAY
Clive Turner,
Freddie Rowe

CINEMATOGRAPHER
Godfrey A. Godar

COMPOSER
David George

CAST
Romy Windsor
(Marie),
Michael T. Weiss
(Richard Adams),
Antony Hamilton
(Tom),
Susanne Severeid
(Janice),
Lamya Derval
(Eleanor),
Norman Anstey
(Sheriff),
Bull Forsche
(Werewolf #1),
Megan Kruskal
(Sister Ruth),
Kate Edwards
(Mrs. Ormstead),
Dennis Folbigge
(Dr. Coombes)

PRODUCTION COMPANY
Allied Vision,
Allied Entertainments
Group PLC

EDITOR
Mac Errington,
Claudia Finkle

SPECIAL EFFECTS
Steve Johnson's
XFX, Inc.

RUNNING TIME
94 min

Howling IV: The Original Nightmare

Terror Unleashed From The Cages of Hell

SYNOPSIS

After experiencing visions of a disturbed nun, author Marie Adams (Romy Windsor) discusses her troubling condition with her doctor, who immediately tells her that her overactive imagination is leading her into some extremely dangerous territory.

With guidance from the doctor, Richard (Michael T. Weiss), Marie's husband decides to take her away from the continued pressure of work and city life for a relaxing break.

Richard locates the perfect getaway for his troubled wife — a cottage in the small town of Drago, some hours from Los Angeles.

Marie travels to Drago with a friend for a much-needed respite, but as the full moon looms closer the author becomes entangled in a mystery and becomes suspicious that something sinister is going on in Drago, something that has razor-sharp claws, throat-ripping teeth, and that kills by the cold light of a full moon.

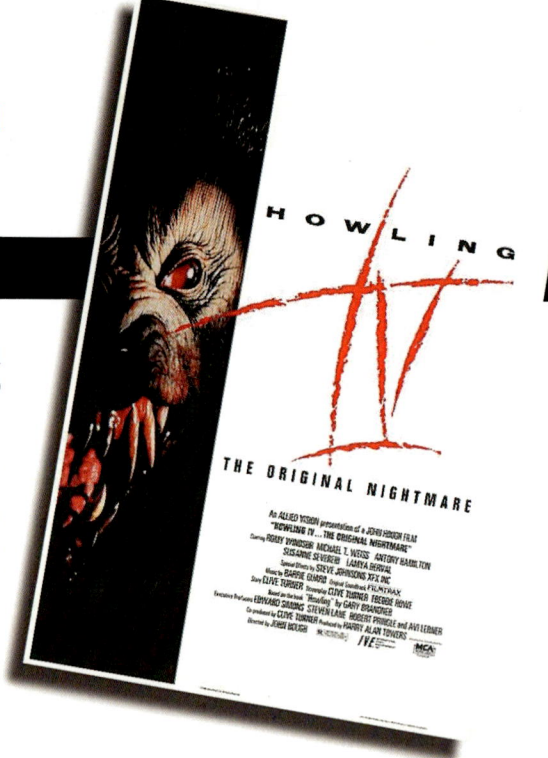

As night descends the Howling jaws of death rise again to shatter the stillness of the night.

Howling IV: The Original Nightmare has been called "tedious", "best and the worst of the first three Howling sequels" and "utterly pointless soft-porn". Yet it is the film's bizarre new levels that provide just enough quirkiness to make this entry in the franchise worth the celluloid it was printed on.

While the film's distributors go to all manner of lengths to claim the entry is the fourth instalment, *Howling IV: The Original Nightmare* is in fact a quasi-remake of *The Howling* on a miniscule budget of $2M.

Like Joe Dante's *The Howling*, this film is another adaptation of Gary Brandner's 1977 novel of the same name but purports to be a more faithful adaptation this time around. That's mostly true, at least to a degree – Freddie Rowe (*Howling V: The Re-Birth*) and Clive Turner's (*The Lawnmower Man*) script does follow the source material more closely, at least more so than Dante's '81 incarnation, which made the conscious decision to leave the soap opera melodrama on the cutting room floor. *Howling IV: The Original Nightmare* deviates from the novel in many respects but tries extremely hard to do so less conspicuously.

The direct-to-VHS feature immediately begins by dropping Brandner's character's lead names (Karen Beatty and Roy) to avoid confusing its target audience with Dante's entry. Karen White is now Marie Adams (Romy Windsor) and her husband Bill Neill is now Richard (Michael T. Weiss).

Clive Turner also gives the story a nip-and-tuck, embellishing many aspects of Brandner's narrative by relocating his female lead's origins to the sprawling Southern California city of Los Angeles. He plumps her up just for good measure with the unique ability of being able to communicate with the dead, which would give *Long Island Medium*, Theresa Caputo, a run for her money, beefing up the

film's running time further with a paranormal subplot. Marie's supernatural ability is soon whitewashed and put down to her simply having an overactive imagination, and with the advice of her doctor Marie and Richard travel to Drago for rest and recuperation.

Another name variation comes in the form of Drago's local gift shop temptress Eleanor (Lamya Derval), previously called Marcia Lura (*The Howling* 1981), who seduces Richard with her large collection of wind chimes, eventually turning Al Bundy (pun intended) into a werewolf.

Another alteration is the absence of a Chris Halloran, who rescues Karyn, arriving with silver bullets which he had made at Karyn's insistence. Instead we are given a badly-executed love triangle between Marie and her publisher, Tom (Antony Hamilton), to fill the void.

The final significant difference between *The Original Nightmare* and Brandner's novel is that in order for freshly-bitten victims to transform into their lupine form they first have to melt into a bloody pool of slime, then reconstitute themselves into wolves. It's these superbly executed moments that shift the film's daytime TV feel up a key, pulling it out of its slump, rescuing it just in time for the credits to roll.

With the previous alternations aside, much of Brandner's novel is retained hereon in – Drago is a peculiar small town (not a resort!), the elderly couple renting the cottage before Marie's arrival mysteriously disappear, and Marie's pet pooch goes missing, only to turn up mauled. The friendly shopkeepers are now renamed the Ormsteads instead of the Jovilets, and we even have a town doctor.

We are also given a version of Inez Polk here, only now she's called Janice Hatch (Susanne Severeid). Janice's print incarnation is an ex-nun and a resident of Pinyon, the town nearest to Drago. Like Inez, Janice left the convent to investigate what happened to her best friend,

MUSIC: THEME SONG

Howling IV: The Original Nightmare's haunting opening track screams 80s from the very moment the tune kicks in, echoing both in style and vein *A Nightmare on Elm Street 4: The Dream Master's*, *Nightmare*, performed by Tuesday Knight, who also replaced Patricia Arquette in the role of Kristen Parker.

Something Evil, Something Dangerous not only serves as the opening song for the fourth instalment of *The Howling* franchise but is additionally the catchiest theme song in the series.

Although never officially released as a single, the track has become a cult hit among *Howling* fans. It was written and performed by Justin Hayward of The Moody Blues, with music by Barrie Guard (*The Toxic Avenger, Part II*). The song rivals leading songs of other big franchises, like Alice Cooper's *Man behind the Mask* (*Friday the 13th Part VI: Jason Lives*) and Dokken's *Dream Warriors* (*A Nightmare on Elm Street 3: Dream Warriors*).

Justin Hayward's track has a repetitive build that pretty accurately teases the slow burn that protagonist Marie and the viewers are about to experience. In addition to *Howling IV: The Original Nightmare*, Hayward has composed and performed for various other film and television shows, including the theme song *It Won't Be Easy* for the 1987 BBC2 science fiction series *Star Cops*, the song *Eternal Woman* for the post-apocalyptic film *She* and music for the animated television series *The Shoe People*.

RETURN OF THE HOWLING

The Nightmare of Drago Prowls Again

The *Howling IV: The Original Nightmare's* final moments falsely promise a continuation to *The Howling V: The Rebirth*. Dr. Coombes (Dennis Folbigge), now a fully-formed werewolf, pounces from the burning inferno at Marie (Romy Windsor) just as the credits roll. Had *The Howling V* continued working from its source material the follow-up would have been very different. Here's what *The Howling V* might have looked like had the producers showed more faith in Gary Brandner's novels.

Three years after the events of *The Howling*, our main protagonist, Karyn Beatty, aka Marie Adams, has now remarried and lives in Seattle. However, Karyn is convinced that the surviving werewolves of Drago have tracked her down. Fearing for the lives of her new family, Karyn leaves town for Mexico, hoping she will lead the evil creatures away from her loved ones.

As the full moon rises, the werewolves return to seek revenge. Can Karyn succumb to her own primal instincts?

The horror begins anew. This is *Return of The Howling*.

Gary Brandner's follow-up novel was released in 1979.

Sister Ruth (Megan Kruskal), who was found wandering in the Drago undergrowth speaking incoherently about the devil, a bell and the sound of howling.

Much of the *Howling IV: The Original Nightmare's* problems do fall at the door of Freddie Rowe (*Howling V: The Re-Birth*) and Clive Turner's (*The Lawnmower Man*) script. Dante wisely chose to inject offbeat humour with lashings of movie references and clever inside jokes to keep the film moving, but *Howling IV: The Original Nightmare* is null and void of any sense of humour and grinds to a halt with the bulk of the film filling its scenery with its cast chewing the fat of the land.

Like the book, *The Original Nightmare* is less quirky than Joe's entry too, and the themes are much less complicated. It's a pretty straightforward story, told in a very straight narrative with added soap opera theatricals. The book, on the other hand, is a fast read, delivering on a great pulp level and creating enough suspense

to keep the pages turning.

Rowe and Turner's take on the book is very literal, committing too firmly to Brandner's narrative, which has too much 'telling' rather than showing, and in doing this the moments that were cut from the film by Turner, Malcolm Burns-Errington (*Cyborg Cop III*) and Claudia Finkle (*Hellbent*) to keep the running time down left key themes with gaping plot holes for the audience to piece together from a jigsaw that had far too many missing pieces unless you had read the source material.

No sooner does the second half kick in than the audience is slipped a jumble of scenes. Janice comes to meet Marie under the pretence that she's Marie's biggest fan, and upon hearing the words "the howling" she is convinced that it has something to do with her friend Sister Ruth, who died before ever being able to explain what happened to her in Drago, where she was found. Much like Sister Ruth, the scenes are incoherent and mismatched.

Upon the film's release Clive Turner dismissed all the blame that was fired point blank into his corner, immediately citing John Hough's direction. Turner stated, "I was disappointed with the director John Hough" from the beginning "but we ended up with a reasonable film."

But one must ask oneself if this was purely sour grapes on Turner's behalf. Prior to cameras rolling Turner was originally pencilled in to direct, but when the film's financiers got wind of this they pulled the plug, and the film, which still hadn't even got a fully fleshed out script, fell into darkness, forcing Turner to hire veteran horror director John Hough at the last minute with what money he had secured.

John accepted the paying gig based on his appreciation for Joe Dante's *The Howling*, his love for the horror genre and a second unexpected career slump. John's previous horror outings, *Eyewitness* (1970) also known as *Sudden Terror*, *Twins of Evil* (1971), *The Legend of Hell House* (1973), *The Incubus* (1982) and *American Gothic* (1987) had been critically well received, so the project seemed the ideal fit for the horror veteran, and John himself at that point was eager to direct a werewolf movie for the first time. However, this all changed, as no sooner had he signed on the dotted line than he realised the production was going to be thwarted from the get-go.

There was no script ready, forcing John, who oversaw the casting, to ask his actors to read monologues and forcing him to rely on his notes thereon in. The budget couldn't even push to filming with sound. All the audio had to be dubbed in during post-production – John was over the project even before he had the chance to call "Action".

Eventually the script was completed and filming commenced at the end of 1987 in South Africa, clumsily posing as California. *Howling IV: The Original Nightmare* was a tough shoot for all involved. John would receive rewrites, notes and messages daily from screen writer Rowe, causing his well-oiled shooting schedule to be thrown into turmoil. On several occasions Hough tried to ask Turner for Rowe's phone number so he could reach out to him, but he was denied direct access. This caused further animosity

between the pair, eventually leading John to suspect Rowe was actually Clive Turner simply trying to make power plays from the side-lines as he wanted to be both producer and director. The tension between the two also made its way onto the set.

One member of the crew, who asked to remain anonymous, stated in an email, "It was an unpleasant atmosphere and experience that put me off working in the industry for many years. I would go as far as to say John Hough was a saint, what he had to put up with was horrendous. That's all I have to say on the film."

The film's final was SFX-heavy and even had the inclusion of squibs for their final on-screen money shot. All of the SFX were created at the XFX, Inc. shop in California, and this was where the preparation and magic of the main werewolf suit occurred before moving the production to Johannesburg, South Africa. The main suit used in the final film's reels was designed and created by Steve Johnson. Bull Forsche was the man in the suit, while Adam Behr was in charge of animatronics. Behr said of his experience working with Johnson and the creature,

THE DIRECTOR: JOHN HOUGH

John Hough was considered by many as a directing force of nature. He took his first job on the 1968 season of *The Avengers*, helming episodes such as *Super Secret Cypher Snatch* and *Homicide and Old Lace*, before moving up the directorial ladder to more meatier jobs that included the TV pilot for a proposed Robin Hood TV show, *Wolfshead:The Legend of Robin Hood*, in 1969.

Sadly, the show hung in pre-production hell and eventually never materialised. The show's pilot was picked up by Hammer Films, which distributed it theatrically.

The film received fairly middle-of-the-road reviews but its marginal success led to Hough being hired to direct an adaptation of Cornell Woolrich's novelette *The Boy Cried Murder*.

Hough's adaptation was released in June 1970 and, much like his previous effort, received an above-average reception from critics.

Hammer, happy with his skills as a director that was able to work to a tight budget, approached him to make the final film in its erotic vampire horror Karnstein Trilogy, *Twins of Evil* (1971).

The film was a huge hit worldwide for Hough, which led to bigger and better productions. But during the late 80s Hough's career began to slide and after *Howling IV: The Original Nightmare* job offers seemed to begin to biodegrade in production budget further.

In 2001 Hough directed his final feature film, *Bad Karma*, which proved too much for producers. It was the final nail in his varied and often colourful career!

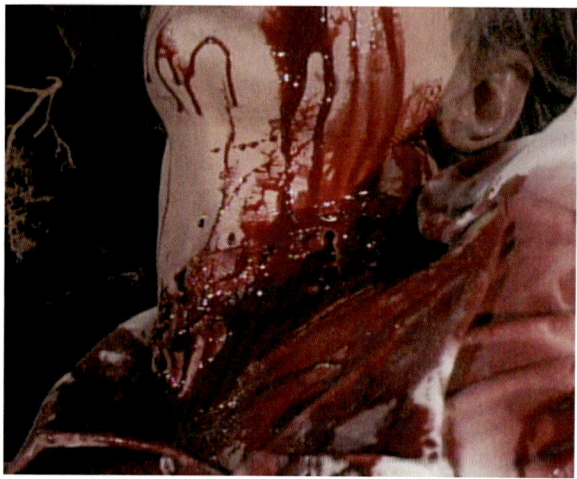

John accepted the paying gig based on his appreciation for Joe Dante's *The Howling*, his love for the horror genre and a second unexpected career slump.

"Steve Johnson was always innovative and uncompromising – in a good way – in his approach to design. I can't think of anything I've seen that came out of that shop that wasn't totally impressive. Some creatures were more puppeteer friendly than others, but when the visual approach to creature effects is as strong as it was from XFX, that's sometimes the way things have to go."

The final scenes were difficult and draining, and the cast and crew spent days on end all huddled under a blanket very close to naked flames. Bull Forsche suffered the worst, buried under layers of the creature suit moving backwards and forwards trying his best to follow direction as mounting tension built to fever pitch from the lighting and camera crew due to the positioning of where the puppeteers needed to be to work the creature correctly.

Once the film finally wrapped, John turned in his version and flew back to England while post-production was being performed in LA. As soon as John stepped off the plane onto British soil Turner immediately went out and filmed several alternative scenes, editing the film to his liking – the vision he had constantly fought John for throughout the production.

One scene Turner left on the cutting room floor involved Susanne Severeid's character's death. "My death scene, where I say the Lord's Prayer while ringing the bell at the end, unfortunately, was cut from the final film," she said. "John Hough really liked it, and it was largely done on the spot. It really came out of the character. It's too bad it was not in the final film."

John was so taken aback by the scene he even contacted Severeid to thank her for her powerful performance, which bought the crew to tears. "I have a letter from him where he said of that scene, "One scene in particular had the crew and myself crying, which is the highest compliment an actress can command," she told me.

Over the years John has distanced himself from *Howling IV: The Original Nightmare* and its problems, and has been known to dismiss questions during interviews about the movie. On several occasions during the writing of this book I have approached John via email for him to take part. All emails have gone unanswered.

Howling IV: The Original Nightmare does manage to achieve a few healthy shocks, but for most of the part the direction is flat, with the story taking far too long to get going – partly down to bad script choices and terrible dialogue. Nevertheless, the film has gone on to gain cult status and even won a Fangoria Golden Chainsaw award for Best Direct-to-Video Feature in 1988. ■

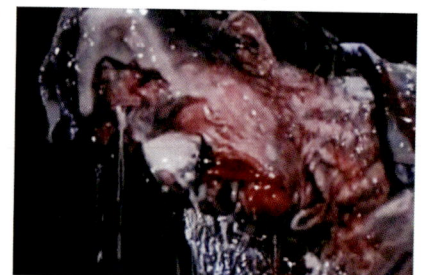
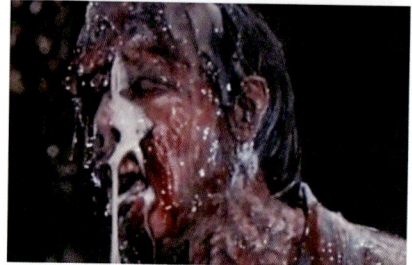
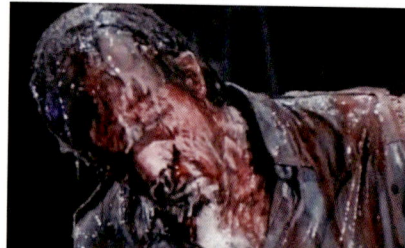

> "There were days where we were puppeteering in a fire set, a group of puppeteers all huddled under a blanket very close to the flames. I remember feeling for Bill Forsche (*Beetlejuice*), who was inside the creature suit rig, and imagining how hot it would be inside it."

greater opportunity to get good scenes. And, let's face it, the audience goes to watch monster movies more for the monsters... although a good script, good acting etc. doesn't hurt either.

ON WHAT HE ENJOYED MOST ABOUT *HOWLING IV: THE ORIGINAL NIGHTMARE*:

I loved the way the transformations worked and the fire scene with the werewolf puppet. I haven't watched the film in quite a while, but in general the thing about puppeteering is that you never get a second chance, or another take just for animatronics, so there's great pressure during shooting to get it right the first time.

ON A POTENTIAL *THE HOWLING* REBOOT:

A lot of the success of those films at the time was because of the creature effects, and I would love to work on the new ones if there's an opportunity. I can only hope that they decide on using live action creatures for some of the work, rather than all CG.

There are some things that puppets do best and some things that computer animation does well, and I feel that some of the greatest creature effects films employ an intelligent mix of both. ■

4.

The Nick Benson interview

Nick Benson's cinematic art has appeared in *The Blob* (1988), *Tremors* (1990) and *A Nightmare on Elm Street 4: The Dream Master* (1988) to name just a few, but it was *Howling IV: The Original Nightmare* where the *Bride of Re-Animator* special effects guru nearly lost an arm.

Working alongside Steve Johnson and the XFX, Inc. crew the talented visual effects artist lay for several hours banging his hand to the ground from under the set built to accommodate Michael T. Weiss's character's melting transformation, eventually cutting off the circulation to Benson's arm before he was rushed off to the hospital.

Unfiltered, Nick discusses stories from the *Howling* trenches and shares his perspective on 80s eye-popping nudity, creature effects and Michael Weiss's love for the make-up chair!

NICK BENSON

ON *THE HOWLING* AND *HOWLING IV* SEQUEL:

I love *The Howling* (1981) and *Howling IV: The Original Nightmare* equally but for different reasons.

The Howling because it was the first and what launched the franchise! *Howling IV: The Original Nightmare* because I was proud to have worked on it and was really happy with what the XFX team had accomplished in this film.

ON NUDITY IN THE SEQUELS AND DEE'S REFUSAL TO REPRISE HER ROLE IN *HOWLING II* BECAUSE OF IT:

Ah Dee... I love that lady, she is just awesome and a phenomenal actress.... BUT as the franchise moved forward, and any 80s horror fan knows... the careful combination of the story, suspense, ghastly imagery, and some eye-popping nudity is what made 80s horror what it was and still is. Iconic!

ON BECOME INVOLVED WITH *HOWLING IV: THE ORIGINAL NIGHTMARE*:

I was roommates with Steve and Steve had stolen me from a theatrical band I was playing in at the time to come and do FX. *Howling IV* was my third film with him and at that time he was a blast to work with and everyone got along famously in his shop, so the environment was always really productive in creating REALLY believable stuff.

I know that all of us put in endless hours of constant research in photos, previous film FX, and LOTS of makeup and FX gag tests.

ON CREATING THE INCREDIBLE MELTING MAN,

WORKING WITH XFX, INC. CREW AND DIRECTOR JOHN HOUGH:

We had fun making some video to send to John Hough in the shop, I know Bill Forsche has video copy of that, we had a lot of fun with John poking fun at his personality.

The wolf suit that Bill wore was one of the largest pieces I worked on for the film. Eric Fielder and I built a "fire" rig in the parking lot of XFX to be used in the scene where the wolf comes through the fire. Additionally, when we shot 2nd unit the melting sequence (puppet) as well as my own arm being used as Michael's once he was melted down pounding my fist on the ground...

"As an FX artist I think all of us in our field know that with more budget, more can be accomplished and that is a given, BUT Steve was a stickler and perfectionist on this within his given budget."

Once the puppet was finished "melting" and Michael's character was mostly liquefied my arm was used as the still human arm grabbing and flailing in mud/muck – the whole sequence was shot next door to XFX on a rented soundstage with a large forest set that was built to accommodate.

We had to call an ambulance from shooting that, as the shoot ran super long and I didn't get a break from under the set and my arm had the circulation cut off.

ON *HOWLING IV: THE ORIGINAL NIGHTMARE*'S BUDGET RESTRAINTS:

I am still quite proud of what was turned out of that shop for the film. It's awesome to hear that Adam was quite happy with it. As an FX artist I think all of us in our field know that with more budget, more can be accomplished and that is a given, BUT Steve was a stickler and perfectionist on this within his given budget.

ON BILL FORSCHE AND THE WEREWOLF SUIT:

AH poor Bill.... he was a true warrior on this set. Someone who could apply makeup to other actors for hours, then climb into that horribly hot suit and get on that crazy dolly we built and spend MORE hours on it. I know Bill F got quite a lot of attention from the ladies,

so I'm sure that made things easier for him on set or should I say "off" haha........

ON HOWLING IV: THE ORIGINAL NIGHTMARE'S SFX STILL HOLDING UP:

I don't think any of us really thought about it holding up this far in the future, I think we just wanted to do the absolute best we could do with what we had at the time and how to constantly push those envelopes to always keep people guessing, "How did they do that?!". Having the team we had with huge talent such as Steve, Bill Corso, Eric Fiedler, Bill Forsche, Tony Rupprecht (Rest in Peace), Bill Barschdorf, Lenny MacDonald and Theresa Burkett really made it feel quite easy to work out how it would all work and work WELL!

ON HOWLING IV: THE ORIGINAL NIGHTMARE'S POLITICS:

I have a vague recollection of the politics side of it... we pretty much stayed out of that and followed the work schedules and tasks requested.

I personally was not affected by any of the struggles between him [John Hough] and Clive.

ON FREDDIE ROWE'S REWRITES BECOMING AN ON-SET PROBLEM:

This would probably be more of a question for Steve Johnson. I was having so much fun doing what I loved and felt no real negativity within this or my end of production (other than Michael Weiss's complaints in makeup and pick-ups). I know nothing of Freddie Rowe. We really had a fun shop and group. Our team always would make the best and most fun even of some darker situations!

ON MICHAEL T. WEISS ALLEGEDLY BEING A PAIN IN THE BUTT:

I won't elaborate on this, but I am sure Bill will LOL.

ON FELLOW CAST/CREW NOT WANTING TO BE ASSOCIATED WITH HOWLING IV: THE ORIGINAL NIGHTMARE:

Personally it's never been erased from my mind (laughing here). It was kind of a gruelling schedule but some pretty unforgettable stuff happened....

I will let Bill tell those stories – there are many, mostly involving him haha

ON JOHN HOUGH'S ALTERNATIVE CUT OF HOWLING IV: THE ORIGINAL NIGHTMARE:

I would love to see a release made of BOTH versions of this film on Blu-ray, both Hough's and Turner's, and let the fans have a say....

ON HOWLING IV: THE ORIGINAL NIGHTMARE'S WEREWOLF AND DOWNTIME:

We LOVED this wolf and the team was very proud.... Steve's design was so menacing in my opinion. We were all very excited to have it look and work the way it did. Downtime? What downtime?? (Clearing throat) drank a lot!

ON HOWLING IV: THE ORIGINAL NIGHTMARE'S RECEPTION:

I think in general the American public at this point was just "over" the franchise and not ready to give it a chance as another film with a slightly different take. I didn't find it boring personally, but I did feel that using a prominent soap opera star [Michael T. Weiss – *Days of Our Lives*] from that time is what made most folks feel it was "soap like" as they were used to seeing the cast in daytime drama as well as that being what the cast was used to performing in.

I still enjoy the film, especially from an FX perspective... I am proud to have been part of that team. ∎

RELEASED
(USA, Feb 22, 1990)

DIRECTOR
Neal Sundstrom

WRITING CREDITS
Gary Brandner
(*The Howling I, II & III*)

STORY
Clive Turner,
Freddie Rowe

SCREENPLAY
Clive Turner

CINEMATOGRAPHER
Arledge Armenaki

COMPOSER
The Factory

CAST
Phil Davis
(Count Istvan),
Victoria Catlin
(Dr. Catherine Peake),
Elizabeth Shé
(Marylou Summers),
Ben Cole
(David Gillespie),
William Shockley
(Richard Hamilton),
Mark Sivertsen
(Jonathan Lane),
Mary Stavin
(Anna)

PRODUCTION COMPANY
Allied Vision

EDITOR
Claudia Finkle,
Bill Swenson,
Neal Sundstrom,
Clive Turner

SPECIAL EFFECTS
Elaine Alexander,
John Axford,
Kevin Brennan,
Mike Elizalde,
János Németh

RUNNING TIME
USA, 98 min,
UK, 96 min

Howling V: The Rebirth
For 500 years the secret lay dormant... Until now!

chilling, heart-racing rollercoaster of fear... The beast has returned!

SYNOPSIS

After being sealed off for over 500 years following a horrific, intentionally staged family mass murder, a mysterious Hungarian castle re-opens its doors with the apparent intention of attracting tourist business. A diverse group of people from different parts of the globe is assembled at the eerie dwelling after having been chosen when they applied for a visa. But once they arrive some begin to wonder if there is more going on than meets the eye. First they hear terrible stories about savage packs of wolves that used to roam the castle grounds and then one by one members of the diverse group begin to disappear, only to be found later with their throats torn out. It soon becomes clear that a murderer is among them, and the culprit may only partially be human.

Howling V: The Rebirth creates a spine-

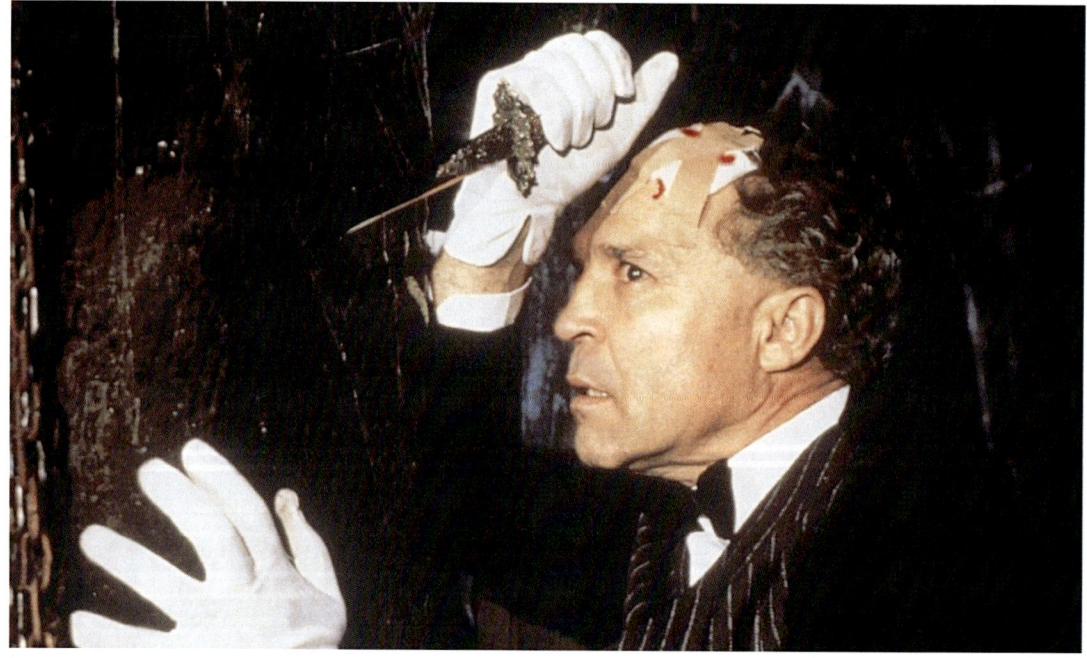

Howling V: The Rebirth is considered by some to be a landmark in cinema of how to make a werewolf movie without an actual werewolf, while others consider it the celluloid incarnation of the Titanic, a grand vehicle not correctly equipped to set sail on its maiden voyage. Then there's the very small minority that praise the film for its likeness to Agatha Christie's *Ten Little Indians* and the YouTube community that "Imagine a Scooby Doo mystery in a haunted house, except for finding a kooky old man in a mask, most of the characters are met with a great big cup of death. That's right; the whole thing is one big lead up without much pay off!" – Allison Pregler, Movie Nights.

Howling V: The Rebirth follows a group of unlucky victims from different walks of life that all converge in a Hungarian castle situated in Budapest for the castle's grand re-opening. The castle, which in all accounts steals the show, had allegedly been sealed for 500 years following a brutal massacre, and when the group arrives and is getting settled in, one by one they are bumped off by an off-screen werewolf until only three are left, just as the full moon rises!

Howling V: The Rebirth's story was carefully crafted by the energetic and enthusiastic Clive Turner, who by this point into his career was well and truly living the rock'n'roll lifestyle embraced by most of the film industry in the late 80s, and coffee wasn't the only stimulant that helped him burn the midnight oil. For the second time the elusive Freddie Rowe (Turner) returned as the writer, while Jan Luce (*My Mom's a Werewolf*) was drafted in as Script Supervisor.

Produced by Gary Barber, Harvey Goldsmith, Steven A. Lane, Robert Pringle, Edward Simons and Clive Turner the film's location moved from South Africa to Hungary.

Unlike *Howling IV: The Original Nightmare*, *Howling V: The Rebirth* had a script prepared well in advance of filming, and after the film's original director left the project due to creative differences, along with the cinematographer (replaced by Arledge Armenaki (*The Slayer*)), Clive Turner had his personal assistant, Vania Phitittas, show his preferred director's film *Tyger Tyger Burning Bright* to his fellow producers in the vain hope they would listen to the problematic wannabe and hire rookie director Neal Sundstrom.

Neal Sundstrom had an almost impossible time directing Elizabeth Shé successfully as the actress's insecurities caused several delays and Sundstrom resorted to handling her with kid gloves.

The Sundstrom family were no strangers to Turner, who had previously worked with Neal's brother Cedric Sundstrom on *Howling IV: The Original Nightmare*, where he performed First Assistant (Director) duties. Once the producers had finally had a chance to view Neal's directorial debut they settled on hiring him and a meeting was quickly arranged to sign him up and ship him off to Budapest to take over the helm of *Howling V: The Rebirth*.

Neal Sundstrom was familiar with the genre, having worked on several low-budget productions such as *Gor II*, *Rage to Kill* and *Space Mutiny*. While none of these films surfed the horror wave their interesting concepts certainly didn't stray far from the *Howling* series path.

Casting was handled by Anthony Barnao (*Re-Animator*), Lisa London (*Leprechaun*) and Estelle Rodkoff (*Troll*) and had almost been completed by the time Sundstrom had fully committed to the project. The producers' insistence on casting genre stars that were recognisable to horror fans and the failure of the previous movie helped provide *Howling V: The Rebirth* with that extra enthusiasm it needed to garner early press coverage and create a buzz around the film's production.

Genre veteran of the eighties, Victoria Catlin (*Ghoulies*, *Maniac Cop*), was cast to play Dr. Catherine Peake, Jill Pearson (*Edge of Sanity*) filled the shoes of Eleanor, while James Bond beauty, Mary Stavin (*House*), took the role of Anna. Other roles were filled with notable TV soap fare but it was the director's ace card, played at the final hour by bringing his close friend and confidant Phil Davis onto the project to play Count Istvan,

that gave the movie its prestigious feel.

Phil Davis was known internationally for roles in the popular BAFTA winning TV drama *Robin of Sherwood*, the feature film *Mr. Quilp* (based on a Charles Dickens novel), *Quadrophenia*, BAFTA winning *The Wall* (Pink Floyd) and the European Film Award-winning *High Hopes*. His screen presence bought an

SCREAM QUEEN: ELIZABETH SHÉ

Elizabeth Shé, who played Marylou Summers, was the film's punch bag upon *Howling V: The Rebirth*'s initial release. Critics slammed Shé for her wooden performance and as time goes by critics have continued to raise an eyebrow or two, but her co-stars remember the overgrown Shirley Temple as "sweet" and a "pretty cool" person, an opinion not shared by *Howling V*'s director, Neal Sundstrom. Sundstrom accused Shé of being "hard work and very insecure", a sentiment shared by a member of crew on *Howling VI: The Freaks*, where Shé made a cameo among the crowed at R.B. Harker's Freak Show. "I don't really remember her other than she was introduced to me as Marylou," the crew member, who asked to remain anonymous in case of upsetting Shé, recalled. "What I do recall was that she was unable to follow instructions quickly and she was very insecure but very beautiful."

Elizabeth Shé has since left the business and during the writing of *The Complete History of The Howling* several attempts were made to reach out to the actress, but all direct contact regarding the book has been rebuffed. Even though the seasons have changed and the years have gone by since *The Rebirth*'s release *The Howling* franchise's very own Shirley Temple hasn't aged a day and we sincerely wish her all the happiness in the world.

extra edge that the series needed to become credible once more, but for every plus to the production there was a minus, and the casting of Elizabeth Shé to play the film's final girl, Marylou Summers, was one of the film's low-blows. Shé, although not unlikeable as a character, couldn't act her way out of a paper bag, a general consensus noted by critics upon the film's release. And then there was Turner's dialogue, which left much to be desired – "the word 'juvenile' comes to mind," stated the director.

The final nail in the coffin of *Howling V: The Rebirth* was the decision not to provide a budget for creature FX. *Howling IV: The Original Nightmare* was every horror fan's candy store if they had bothered to stick around long enough for Steve Johnson and his amazing crew to do their thing – no matter what critics or armchair reviewers had to say the tremendous work and effort that came out of Johnson's XFX, Inc. workshop was mindblowing.

Howling V: The Rebirth had to make do with the odd jugular throat tear here and there, with almost all of the kills conducted off-screen or out of shot. Steve Johnson, however, came to the film's rescue earlier on by loaning *Howling IV*'s iconic beast suit for use on Sundstrom's film. "When I first saw the werewolf I thought they were joking," stated Sundstrom. "He was haggard and not convincing at all ... Cheap and looked like he had done a movie or 4."

Sundstrom, not being a pushover, refused to use the suit in any major scenes unless the creature was shot in the shadows. "There was no wiring and a person would have had to climb into the suit and perform," he added, which in fact was a task Bill Forsche had to undertake during the making of *Howling IV: The Original Nightmare* – without complaint.

Once the cast and crew arrived on location in Budapest filming commenced, almost without a hitch, but due to Hungary being a socialist country, for every foreign crew member Sundstrom had to have at least two locals. This made for a larger crew than he had expected and much of his direction was lost in translation.

Clive Turner didn't disappoint in the drama department and proved to be a problem yet again, but this time he had given himself a much larger role in the film, moving up the thespian ladder from a bit-part contribution (Tow Truck Driver) in *Howling IV: The Original Nightmare* to Ray Price, the film's comic relief, in *Howling V: The Rebirth*. With Turner's ability to rub almost anybody up the wrong way tempers soon began to fray and Sundstrom snapped, firing the film's key grip. Sundstrom had an almost impossible time directing Elizabeth Shé successfully as the actress's insecurities caused several delays and Sundstrom resorted to handling her with kid gloves.

When filming had eventually wrapped and the cast and crew had flown back to home territory, the editing process began and Turner promptly brought in his own editor, Claudia Finkle (*Beverly Hills Cop II*), to cut the film to his liking without Sundstrom's participation, which was becoming something of a habit. John Hough had previously been shut out of the editing suite on *Howling IV: The Original Nightmare* and was left devastated by the final cut of the film that had his name above the title.

This time around Turner courteously invited Sundstrom to come in and view his final cut. Sundstrom was unhappy with what he saw and after many hours of going back and forth he eventually convinced Turner to let him have a go at editing the film he had been hired to direct. Turner grudging agreed, so Sundstrom and Bill Swenson (*Lena's Holiday*) got to work.

The film's musical direction ditched the 80s rock theme that had become synonymous with

the franchise since the 1985 sequel in favour of a more grandiose sound composed by The Factory, whose work included *Gomer Pyle: USMC*.

Howling V: The Rebirth was officially released by International Video Entertainment in the United Kingdom in 1992, derived from its earlier release on February 22, 1990 in the USA (contrary to the ever-reliable Wikipedia information). Much like the previous movie, the film's release strategy was scatter gunned like a shower of bullets throughout the decades, with little to no marketing.

The marketing campaign predominately focused on the "decrepit" and "unusable" werewolf from the fourth instalment and pushed the selling point that, just like *Nightmare on Elm Street* and *Friday the 13th*, the *Howling* series continued to deliver top video rental sales due to it being a premium name in horror, and that it was this cleverly thought-out and well-orchestrated attack that brought punters into the rental stores to check out the latest instalment in the ever-breeding series.

Howling V: The Rebirth performed better than anyone expected and critics, while still split down the middle, did find moments of enjoyment in the film over its predecessors, noting its similarities to *Ten Little Indians* and *The Beast Must Die*. To date *Howling V: The Rebirth* holds an audience score of 25%, with an average rating of 2.6/5 on Rotten Tomatoes – an improvement when compared to *Howling IV: The Original Nightmare*.

Howling V: The Rebirth was finally released on DVD as a double feature with *Howling VI: The Freaks* on September 23, 2003 by Artisan Home Entertainment and once again they reused the "haggard" werewolf to push the title onto consumers. In 2007 the double feature was repackaged and released by Timeless Media Group. ∎

5.

The Neal Sundstrom interview

Howling V: The Rebirth was dropped direct-to-video during the VHS landfill month of February 1990, where little of value could be found on video rental shelves other than disastrous productions. Studios wanted to put behind them as quickly as they could, with minimal fallout, low-budget horror fare that was considered uncool for school and had no place among the big boys of summer. Vehicles with D-grade budgets and fading stars, that carried B-grade chills and thrills and didn't quite cut the mustard, were shuffled into the Direct-to-VHS nether realm – films screwed royally by the studio that only got to see the light of day due to contractual obligation, movies that were later sold on to broadcasting stations to fill the late-night graveyard shift less than three months into their initial release.

Filmed in Budapest, *Howling V: The Rebirth* fitted all of the dump month criteria but managed to dodge the Super Bowl bullet and bypass, by a mere two days, Presidents' Day another day, calendar dates of February known to suppress spending habits on movies.

Neal Sundstrom, who was co-director of *Space Mutiny* was hired to steer the ship when his brother, Cedric Sundstrom (*Howling IV: The Original Nightmare* First Assistant Director, Second Unit Director), declined the offer of directing the fifth instalment in the series. Neal's efforts provided another interesting outing in the *Howling* franchise canon and here's what the *Slash* (2002) director had to say on his entry in the series that was still no closer to solving its conceptual challenges five movies on.

NEAL SUNDSTROM

ON BECOME INVOLVED WITH *HOWLING V: THE REBIRTH*, AND NEAL SUNDSTROM'S OPINION OF THE SCRIPT:

The American producers had seen my film *Tyger Tyger Burning Bright* through Clive Turner's personal assistant, Vania Phitittas. At the time I was living in London and they requested a meeting. We met in Soho and after a brief chat they offered me to go to Budapest to take over the helm.

They had been in principal photography for just over a week and things were not working out. I was young, keen for adventure and accepted immediately – script unseen.

When I first read the script I found the plot ok – however, the dialogue left a lot to be desired. The word 'juvenile' comes to mind.

ON FILLING THE SHOES OF A CAPTAIN WHO DIDN'T STAY LONG ENOUGH TO GET THE SHIP TO PORT:

The condition for me taking over the film was simple and straightforward ... Let me do my job ... And for the most part Clive obliged. I think he had no choice as the American producers loved my film *Tyger Tyger*, and possibly Clive's history of interfering ... We could never agree on his script and so I stopped trying and did what I thought was best.

Indians whodunit.

INSPIRATIONS FOR NEAL SUNDSTROM'S STYLE OF SHOOTING:
Once I had seen the creature and made the decision to not feature it I was inspired by *Rosemary's Baby* and *Ten Little Indians*.

LOCATION, LOCATION, LOCATION:
Although there were no location specific problems at all, we were shooting in Budapest – which was a socialist country – and so for every foreign crew member we had at least two locals. This made for a large crew. Some things did get lost in translation but for the

ON IMDB'S RUMOURS IT WAS CEDRIC SUNDSTROM WHO ABANDONED *HOWLING V: THE REBIRTH* BEFORE SHOOTING:
Cedric abandoned *Howling IV*. He had nothing to do with this film!

ON THE BIG BOSS, CLIVE TURNER:
Clive was the boss for sure. When I met him I found him to be energetic, enthusiastic and committed to the *Howling* series. Bear in mind this was the 1980s and the Rock'n'Roll lifestyle was embraced by most of the film industry, with Clive leading the charge.

He was a large, supercharged personality and definitely did try to control every aspect of the film. I was young, arrogant and wanted things my way. This could have been a recipe for disaster. But somehow we two hard-headed individuals managed to actually enjoy the process and each other. We often argued over the script and eventually I realized that just doing my own thing was the way to go.

ON *HOWLING V: THE REBIRTH*'S VISUAL GOAL:
Everything changed when the FX department introduced me to the 'Creature'. I think my exact words were, "You are f***ing kidding me! You cannot be serious!" It was old, haggard, comical, and had already done a movie or 6. I immediately knew that I had to show as little of the creature as possible.

I decided to turn the film into a *Ten Little*

most part the crew were professional.

[But] I loved filming in Budapest. I used the castle for inspiration. The dye had been set on my arrival in design and dressing.

ON CLIVE TURNER'S BERATING:
Clive was exhausting, and more than anything else he was energy-sapping. He would make nonsensical suggestions and I realized very early on that he actually did not know what he did not know when it came to directing and the creative process. Not only did this dance waste a lot of time, which we had little of, but it was very frustrating. I cannot even imagine how many times a day I must have rolled my eyes.

Eventually he left me alone and stopped coming to the set.

ON *HOWLING V: THE REBIRTH*'S ORIGINAL

CINEMATOGRAPHER ABANDONING SHIP AND FIRING THE FILM'S KEY GRIP:

I have no recollection of any other DOP other than Arledge. Perhaps the original cinematographer left with the original director. I had nothing to do with this.

I did, however, fire the key grip, who at every turn tried to block my ideas. Everything I asked of him was a problem, every camera move he questioned and I believe my youth and energy offended him. I then brought in my own key grip from South Africa and production continued.

ON STEVE JOHNSON SPEAKING OUT ABOUT THE PRODUCERS NEVER RESERVING A BUDGET FOR THE SFX AND LOANING *HOWLING IV: THE ORIGINAL NIGHTMARE*'S WEREWOLF SUIT:

When I first saw the werewolf I thought they were joking ... He was haggard and not convincing at all ... Cheap and looked like he had done a movie or 4 ... That is why you seldom see the creature in the movie ... I turned the script into *Ten Little Indians* and used the creature sparingly ... No budget at all for SFX.

The suit was decrepit and unusable. I was told categorically that this was the creature I was to use. There was no wiring and a person would have had to climb into the suit and perform. As you see in the film, I avoided this as best I could!

ON WORKING WITH SUCH A LARGE CAST:

Working with such a large cast was not without its challenges. I was young, unknown and had very specific ideas on performances.

ON HOW EASY IT WAS TO DIRECT THE CAST:

The first week was very tough. It took the cast a while to realize that I was not going to be bullied by them. That, although young, I knew what I wanted and I would not be intimidated! Once this was established it got easier and they began to trust me.

ON ELIZABETH SHÉ, AKA MARYLOU:

She was hard work and very insecure.

ON DIRECTING *ALIEN 3*'S PHIL DAVIS:

Phil Davis is a friend of mine. I hired Phil Davis. I felt that I needed a great actor and it was a way for me to assert my creative authority.

Phil and I have an interesting history as he was once engaged to my then wife, Kitty Aldridge.

ON BEING KIDNAPPED:

At the time that we were filming in Budapest, *Nightmare on Elm Street* was filming there too. The director was staying at the same hotel as I and we were both sent cars to drive us to our respective sets in the morning. Both cars were identical and one morning we mistakenly got into the wrong cars.

En route I noticed that the landscape was unfamiliar. The driver did not speak English and lack of sleep, exhaustion and my fertile imagination led me to believe that I was possibly being kidnapped. This was the Cold War era after all!

I let out a huge sigh of relief when we arrived at our destination – the film set of Freddy Krueger. I assume their director had a very similar experience.

ON THE FILM'S EDITING:

Originally Clive and his editor cut the film without my participation.

Clive invited me to come and have a look at the edit ....

I eventually convinced him to let me have a go – with this editor – and the film you see is the cut the two of us did.

WHEN CAMERAS WENT DOWN:

Budapest was a party. Even though we were behind the Iron Curtain, we certainly had fun. But as you know, "what happens on set, stays on set". ■

The Mark Sivertsen interview

Mark Sivertsen is probably better known for his recurring roles in daytime TV's *The Bold and the Beautiful*, *Passions* and *Highway to Heaven*, but in the last half of the 80s the jobbing actor found himself cast as Jonathan Lane in *Howling V: The Rebirth*.

The first half of the 1980s saw four *Howling* films released at the rate of almost one a year, and all had been commercially rewarding. But, following the depressed critical greeting of 1988's *The Original Nightmare*, no-one involved with the series could deny that the franchise needed a revamp, a gut-punch, and with that Clive Turner once again began the monumental task of rewriting *The Howling* history with full creative freedom.

With the exuberant young director, Neal Sundstrom, hired, filming commenced. In his own words Mark Sivertsen, *The Last Stand* actor, looks back at his time spent filming in Budapest, the Budapest ladies and Budapest food for your reading pleasure!

MARK SIVERTSEN

ON BEING CAST AS JONATHAN LANE IN *HOWLING V: THE REBIRTH*:

It was a straight audition through my agent. Interesting though, I do remember I had a fever of 104 and I felt awful, so I took an apple with me to eat during the audition. It provided a distraction from the fever. Maybe it helped me get the job.

But to me it's just another horror film. But in saying that, I guess I was always interested in werewolf films.

ON HIS CHARACTER:

I played a tennis pro. I play a lot of tennis, especially back then, so it fitted seamlessly.

ON REWATCHING THE PREVIOUS MOVIES BEFORE FILMING *HOWLING V: THE REBIRTH*:

No, I didn't bother with the other instalments.

ON FILMING IN BUDAPEST:

It was interesting. I believe the country was much different from how it is now.

The food was terrible. Coming from California, where we have everything to choose from, eating it was horrible. They boil everything. I do remember, however, that the women were surprisingly beautiful.

ON HIS THOUGHTS OF HOW THE FILM TRANSLATED FROM PAGE TO FILM:

I think it translated well. There were re-writes, but with most films you get re-writes.

ON THE "DECREPIT AND UNUSABLE" WEREWOLF SUIT:

I don't [recall]. There definitely was a lack of

> "My fun was coming back to the hotel and getting a massage. I believe it cost me ten dollars. There was nothing else really to do there. I love travel, so getting another location job was exciting."

ON HOW THE LARGE CAST GOT ALONG AND HIS THOUGHTS ON ELIZABETH SHÉ, AKA MARYLOU:
We got along well. It was fun. I do remember her (Elizabeth Shé) being pretty cool.

ON HIS INITIAL THOUGHTS AFTER WATCHING *HOWLING V: THE REBIRTH* FOR THE FIRST TIME:
I did not see it for a while after I wrapped. I was working so much then. I was happy with the end result.

HIS FAVOURITE MEMORIES OF FILMING IN BUDAPEST:
The beautiful parts of Budapest and the wonderful catacombs underneath the whole city were fascinating. And of course, the beautiful women!

ONCE THE CAMERAS WENT DOWN:
My fun was coming back to the hotel and getting a massage. I believe it cost me ten dollars. There was nothing else really to do there. I love travel, so getting another location job was exciting. ■

a werewolf in the film. As actors we routinely work with nothing, more so nowadays. Sometimes we worked with a production assistant in place of an actor, so it was not that hard. It's part of the game. I do obviously prefer having an actor there.

Howling VI: The Freaks

Vampire vs. Werewolf: The Ultimate Clash of the Forces of Evil...

RELEASED
(UK, Apr 18, 1991)

DIRECTOR
Hope Perello

WRITING CREDITS
Gary Brandner
(*The Howling I, II & III*)

STORY
Kevin Rock

SCREENPLAY
Kevin Rock

CINEMATOGRAPHER
Edward J. Pei

COMPOSER
Patrick Gleeson

CAST
Brendan Hughes (Ian),
Michele Matheson (Elizabeth),
Sean Sullivan (Winston),
Antonio Fargas (Bellamey),
Carol Lynley (Miss Eddington),
Bruce Payne (R.B Harker)

PRODUCTION COMPANY
Allied Entertainments Group PLC

EDITOR
Adam Wolfe,
Hope Perello,
Clive Turner

SPECIAL EFFECTS
Todd Masters,
Steve Johnson

RUNNING TIME
108 min

SYNOPSIS

Set in the barren rural town of Canton Bluff, the story centres on the enigmatic figure of Ian (Brendan Hughes), a likable but severely solitary drifter who takes a job making repairs to the local church. Eschewing human contact, Ian seems unnaturally leery of the impending full moon, a fear shared by a man named Harker (Bruce Payne), the owner of a sleazy travelling carnival. Aware that Ian is a genuine werewolf, Harker is able to blackmail the young man into working for his carnival, where he is put on display with other human oddities. To further complicate matters, Harker is revealed to have a monstrous secret of his own – he's a vampire, who sees Ian's condition as a cover for preying on the blood of local folk.

Howling VI: The Freaks is the ultimate clash

of the forces of Evil Vampire vs Werewolf, man vs beast!

Howling V: The Rebirth proved to be a marginal success on VHS and while the film regenerated some interest in the series it was also a perfectly respectable end, both visually (location and sets) and creatively, to a storyline that critics complained was so thin it could hardly support the film's over inflated running time, let alone any legitimate follow-up.

Of course, the prospect of wringing a few more dollars out of *The Howling* cash cow was difficult for the film's producers

Hope Perello, the only female director to grace the series, was satisfied she had done her best on such a low budget and tight schedule and this opinion was shared by all involved but one.

to ignore and even though the viewing public, who were sufficiently satiated by sequels and had begun to seek more aesthetically interesting movies with solid storytelling, *Howling*'s team of producers were eager to release another *Howling* quickie to line their pockets. For the second time in the series history *Howling VI* was creatively lacking, a ship without a captain due to the earlier director leaving over creative differences.

Tyrant, writer, producer, actor and "on-set drug dealer" Clive Turner (*Howling IV: The Original Nightmare* and *Howling V: The Rebirth*) took a short break from his role of wearing multiple job titles on *Howling VI: The Freaks* to focus all his attention on another more pressing matter, *The Lawnmower Man*, a film that had found itself in a continued cycle of mishaps. New Line Cinema had obtained the rights to Stephen King's short story of the same name and instead of hiring a

team of writers to create a script based on his work New Line Cinema simply attached an unrelated script called *Cyber God* by the film's director Brett Leonard (*Hideaway*) and Second Unit Director Gimel Everett (*Man-Thing*) to the name.

Stephen King, the iconic horror author, who regained full licenses for his movies *The Dead Zone, Cujo, Creepshow, Children of the Corn, Cat's Eye* and *Firestarter* (September 1, 2018), was furious at his name being used on a completely unrelated story he had nothing to do with and began legal action against the studio to have his name removed from *The Lawnmower Man* and its future promotional material.

With Turner out of the picture a writer by the name of Kevin Rock (*Warlock: The Armageddon*) was hired. When signing up for the production he was informed his script duties would carry over two films, *Howling VI: The Freaks* and *Howling VII*, which would begin filming early 1992. Rock, with very little insight into the *Howling* sequels, drew inspiration from Gary Brandner's third novel, *The Howling III: Echoes*, and developed his story around a drifter who comes to town to escape his past. This was a similar angle to that which Philippe Mora had gone for in *Howling III: Marsupials*, but on the flip side Rock made sure he stripped the series right back to basics, removing all of comedic tone from later entries, and addressed *Howling* fans' concerns with the series so far. Once the script had been completed Richard Reams, who had been brought on board by producers Steve Lane and Bob Pringle as Production Designer, was asked to nip and tuck Rock's high-concept script so *Howling VI: The Freaks* could shoot in Los Angeles. After several days reviewing Rock's material both production designer and writer worked around the $1 million budget to make it happen, ditching Turner's preferred location of Budapest.

Hope Perello (*Dolls*) eventually filled the shoes of the absent director. She had previously worked as a Second Unit Director on David Schmoeller's *Puppetmaster* for Charles Band and her keenness for progressing to Director landed her the job on *Howling VI: The Freaks*. "I was helping them with the budget [after Turner's enforced absence by the other producers]," Perello said. "The director they had planned to hire didn't work out. I told them my ideas for the script revisions and they liked what I said and hired me."

Perello met with Rock at a close friend's home and both began to develop Rock's already solid first draft, building on the duality of the werewolf's character, Ian, and his battle between the light and dark side of his nature. Perello, after reading Rock's script prior to meeting him, began to research past and present exhibitions of freak shows, freaks, monstrosities and the marvels of nature that were all essential components of the

THE TWISTED PLAYHOUSE: THE FREAKS

Howling VI: The Freaks' central setting was a travelling Freak Show. In the mid-16th century such shows did indeed exist and, as seen in the film, they were extremely popular pastimes. While often thought of as exploitative, degrading and cruel, most reports paint a picture of headlining exhibits being both accepted and well-paid by the circus staff. In many cases the performers not only out-earned everyone in the audience, but also their own very own Freak Show promoters. Any mistreatment generally came from the public, who did not look at the performers as people but more as objects to ridicule for their biological rarities.

Sideshow acts were not always born different; sometimes they were manufactured to bring in additional money from the crowds when takings were down. Freak Show promoters would take any peculiar-looking person, whose familiarity to those around them made for acceptance, and play up that peculiarity, adding a good backstory, so that they had a fresh attraction.

Fedor Jeftichew, also known as Jo-Jo the Dog-Faced Boy, was R.B Harker's answer to Ian. Born Fedor Jeftichew in 1868, Jo-Jo the Dog-Faced Boy was a famed freak show performer from Russia, brought to the USA at the age of 16. Jeftichew was born with hereditary hypertrichosis (also known as werewolf syndrome), which causes an excessive amount of hair growth over the entire body.

Described as being as playful as a puppy with his audiences, and "the most absorbingly interesting curiosity to ever reach American shores", died of pneumonia on January 31, 1904 in Greece at just 35.

travelling exhibitions in Europe and America throughout the Victorian period. "I loved the pathos that is elicited by people who are handicapped in this way," she stated. Gradually the duo built these aspects into what Rock already had until both parties were happy with what was down on paper. Then the arduous task was now to bring it all to life with Caroline Sax (*Howling II: Your Sister Is a Werewolf*) supervising the script's proceedings.

Casting for the movie fell into two camps. Richard Reams brought on board set decorator Simon Dobbin (*Bring It On: All or Nothing*), costume designer Lynn Murdock (*Roundhouse*) and FX artists Todd Master (*A Nightmare on Elm Street 5: The Dream Child*) and the XFX, Inc. team, run and owned by Steve Johnson (*Night of the Demons 2*). Filling the principal cast was sub-contracted and Sean Sullivan (*Back to the Future Part III*), Michele Matheson (*Kingpin*), Bruce Payne (*Warlock III: The End of Innocence*) and Deep Roy (*Return to Oz*) were all hired. The role of Ian, the sympathetic werewolf, went to Brendan Hughes, who had previously worked un-credited on *An American Werewolf in London*.

When the movie began shooting everyone pulled together to make what they had work. It was a real family atmosphere on set and there were only a few minor setbacks, which came in the form of having various exterior forces on set that unintentionally got in the way of filming, causing delays that eventually led to the film running out of time and money to shoot the slow-build pay off Werewolf vs Vampire. But to create an authentic Freak Show, like the one run by R.B Harker (Bruce Payne) in *Howling VI: The Freaks*, called for the use of animal actors. Freak Shows often exhibited animals alongside their human counterparts, with extreme size or the perfection of the miniature being desirable features. The film's aesthetics needed to be on the money, so throughout the scenes that featured animals the American Humane Association had to be on set to oversee all animal action and enforce their strict guidelines for the safe use of animals, intervening if necessary if any animal was deemed to be in distress. Eventually the American Humane Association oversaw a significant amount of filming and left the set satisfied. The production was in compliance with their guidelines and the film was later rated acceptable.

Editing began as soon as the film was in the can. Perello assisted the film's editing alongside editor Adam Wolfe (*Watchers II*). When Perello's cut was complete she handed it in accompanied by Patrick Gleeson's (*Deadly Illusion*) score. Perello, the only female director to grace the series, was satisfied she had done her best on such a low budget and tight schedule and this opinion was shared by all involved but one. No sooner had Perello's back been turned than Clive Turner got comfy in his favourite chair in the editing suite and began removing Perello's choice of music in favour of his own.

Howling VI: The Freaks was sold to several distributors. The landscape had changed

dramatically since the release of *Howling V: The Rebirth* and horror wasn't the leading genre on rental aisles. To make timing even more unfavourable, *Howling VI: The Freaks* was about to hit the market at around about the same time as two genre heavyweights, *Child's Play 3* and *Freddy's Dead: The Final Nightmare*.

On April 18, 1991 *Howling VI: The Freaks* was released in the UK and on June 13, 1991 USA finally got their turn to see the finished film. While *Howling VI: The Freaks* managed to dodge the dump months' often fatal bullet the movie failed to live up to the producers' expectations and *The Freaks* struggled to generate interest even by word of mouth.

The film's critical reception was moderate to positive with high praise going to XFX, Inc. For their retro style transformation of Ian, which harked back to David Naughton's character David Kessler in *An American Werewolf in London*. Kevin Rock was also favoured for his craft and intelligent screenplay and both the carnival setting and Alligator Boy (Sean Gregory Sullivan) became firm favourites for critical praise, but there was no movement on the VHS charts and *The Freaks* remained a low priority for horror fans.

1991 turned out to be a dull year for film releases, with the exception of the sleeper hit *Silence of the Lambs*, which was released theatrically one month after *Howling VI: The Freaks* and gained widespread success and critical acclaim. Producers Steve Lane and Bob Pringle were displeased by *Howling VI: The Freaks*' performance and plans to shoot *Howling VII* were scrapped. Kevin Rock went on to pen another studio bomb, the extremely underrated *Warlock: The Armageddon* for Trimark Pictures.

Howling VI: The Freaks looked as if it had finally brought the franchise to its natural end due to its poor reception but Clive Turner, who had been forced into the background on *Howling VI: The Freaks*, was not having any of it, and he gave birth to one ugly son of a bitch with real bad taste in line dancing – he gave us *Howling: New Moon Rising*!!! ∎

6.

The Hope Perello interview

By the end of 1990 the heyday of the horror sequels was already in sharp decline. *Initiation: Silent Night, Deadly Night 4*, *Prom Night III: The Last Kiss*, *Slumber Party Massacre III* and *Sorority House Massacre II* all failed to make any real dent in the video store cash registers, yet studios continued to greenlight any film that had any form of association with an already established franchise, no matter how tenuous the connection.

Nary had a week gone by than a remotely-marketable revamped franchise quickie wasn't released that simply imitated the previous film with a slight variation of the same regurgitation. *The Amityville Curse*, Claudio Fragasso's *House 5* and *Troll 2* were all pushed out onto an unsuspecting marketplace, and 1991 continued the trend.

Producers right from the trunk of their car on Skid Row to the highest paid studio executive on Washington Blvd. continued to milk their franchise cash cow, and that same year *Alligator II: The Mutation*, *Omen IV: The Awakening* and *Silent Night, Deadly Night 5: The Toy Maker* filled a declining gap in the market and *Howling VI: The Freaks* followed suit.

Directed by Hope Perello, from the screenplay by Kevin Rock, and starring Brendan Hughes, Bruce Payne, Michele Matheson and Sean Gregory Sullivan, the sixth entry in the series was released with barely any multimedia advertising, and while by no means a VHS blockbuster, it successfully brought promise with its werewolf vs. vampire showdown.

Hope Perello, who is now a full-time advocate for the arts and arts education, talks about *Howling VI*'s budget limitations, the obligation to deliver entertainment and the producers tampering with the film's score! Here's to the memories...

HOPE PERELLO

FROM EMPIRE PICTURES TO FULL MOON FEATURES AND THE ALLIED ENTERTAINMENT GROUP:

The movies I worked on with Charlie Band's company, Empire, and then Full Moon, were different in that they were lower budget, but my experience with those films is what led to getting the job to direct *The Howling VI*. I was helping them with the budget and then the director they had planned to hire didn't work out. I told them my ideas for the script revisions and they liked what I said and hired me.

I didn't really like horror films but I jumped at the chance to direct my first film, especially one that had an intriguing set up like this one did.

ON THE PRESSURE OF COMING ONBOARD AN ALREADY ESTABLISHED FRANCHISE:

I wanted to make independent dramas, not horror films, so I knew I was going to do the film differently than others from Joe Dante or the other directors. I set out to do something a bit more unique, but still felt obligated to deliver entertainment to the audience.

ON DEVELOPING THE SCRIPT WITH KEVIN ROCK (*WARLOCK: THE ARAMGEDDON*):

I did have input on the script. I thought Kevin Rock had written an interesting story, but he and I got a chance to do some further development. We went to a house that a friend of mine had vacated temporarily because of a job and worked on it together. I was very much drawn to the duality of the werewolf character, the battle between the light and dark sides of his nature. And I was very interested in making the most of the freak show aspect of the story's setting. I did a lot of research about the look and feel of the type of people who worked in those type of shows, and I loved the pathos that is elicited by people who are handicapped in this way. I also like the idea of a small town girl being drawn to the dark and tortured Ian, and how the religious fervor of the town created drama and tension.

ON BRINGING *HOWLING VI: THE FREAKS* TO LIFE:

As the woman in charge I would say that I just treated this film as if it wasn't a genre film. I used references to the Italian director Antonioni and the Russian writer Dostoevsky when talking to people about its themes. We also set out to hire talented actors like Bruce Payne and Sean Sullivan, and great special effects people like Steve Johnson and Todd Masters. We tried to push the envelope a bit and do something different with the effects. It wasn't always successful but I think considering the budget those two guys did a great job.

The key to a good film is typically hiring really good people and I do think everyone was working very hard to make the film look interesting and have the story hold together.

ON THE REASON BEHIND *HOWLING VI*'S SLOW

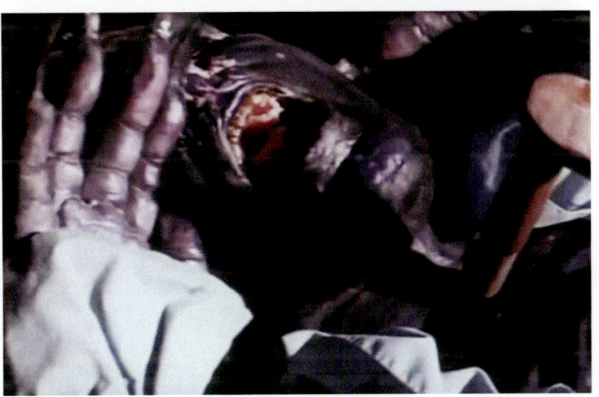

BUILD-UP:

We did the slow build on purpose. I was inspired by classics like *The Exorcist* and *The Omen*, films in which nothing much happens in the first half hour so that you get to know the characters, and then when bad things start happening to them you really care. We did make a concerted effort to create mystery and suspense though at the very beginning, with the girl being chased through the orange grove and attacked. We thought that would create a sense of danger that then allowed us to have that be the "bomb under the table", a plot device Hitchcock referred to.

ON *HOWLING VI: THE FREAKS* METAPHOR AND COMMENTARY:

As I mentioned before, I feel that the film illustrated a man's battle with his own nature, with darker forces, such as Harker, playing to Ian's darker side. It was interesting to delve into whether fate determines the choices you make. The film also allowed us to see how society's vulnerable populations, like the "freaks" in the carnival, are drawn to those, like the carnival owner Harker, who

"I was inspired by classics like *The Exorcist* and *The Omen*, films in which nothing much happens in the first half hour so that you get to know the characters, and then when bad things start happening to them you really care. We did make a concerted effort to create mystery and suspense though at the very beginning, with the girl being chased through the orange grove and attacked. We thought that would create a sense of danger that then allowed us to have that be the "bomb under the table", a plot device Hitchcock referred to."

prey on their weaknesses. There are always people who are considered "freaks" in our society, outcasts, people who are different, and I was very drawn to these characters in the story, wanting to show their struggles and their desire to become accepted in the world.

ON STORIES FROM *HOWLING VI: THE FREAKS* TRENCHES:

Need to try to remember... I think it was pretty wild on the set when it came to doing the Freaks – Antonio Fargas, who had played "Huggy Bear" in *Starsky and Hutch*, had to look like he bit the head off a live chicken. And we had to add a fake boob to the hermaphrodite, and small fake arm to the dwarf actor Deep Roy.

But I also remember trying to get avant-garde composer Harold Budd to do the music for the film. He watched it and said, "No thanks." I don't think he realized it was a horror movie about a werewolf and a vampire. He had no idea what to do with it.

ON PRODUCERS' INTERFERENCE:

I did an edit of the film with music that I had chosen and one of the producers took over the film and added his own choices in some parts of the film.

ON *HOWLING VI: THE FREAKS* ENDING:

The ending of the film is a bit ridiculous. We ran out of time to do it effectively and the story points were only there to lead to another sequel, which I felt did not make it a very successful ending for the film.

ON *HOWLING VI: THE FREAKS* COMPLETED VISION:

The film was very much my vision, with the exception of some of the musical choices made by one of the producers, so the film was what I had planned it be, with the obvious limitations of budget and time.

ON BEING TYPECAST AS A GENRE DIRECTOR:

It was hard to get people to think of you for different types of films after I directed *Howling VI*. It was also hard because, being a woman, a lot of people didn't want a woman director. And that hasn't really changed all that much. But doing the film allowed me to

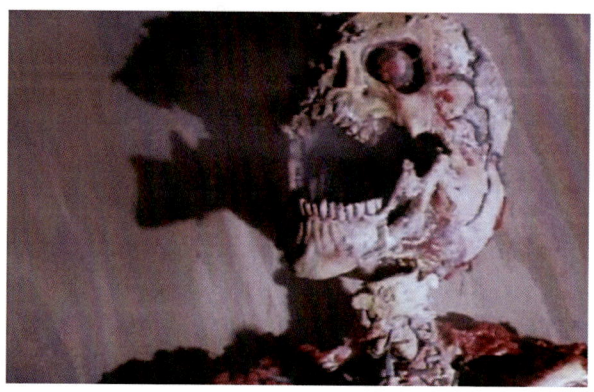

learn a lot and did give me confidence the next time I got the chance to direct. ∎

6.

The Richard Reams interview

Howling VI: The Freaks, directed by Hope Perello, was a visual treat for the franchise that had seen a varying degree of quality since its conception in 1981.

While *Howling VI: The Freaks* was no brisk chiller to revive audiences' interest in the flagging werewolf sub-genre it offered broad strokes of unique colour and angles to a series that had become nothing more than a cannon fodder cash cow.

With Clive Turner's departure from the series as script writer and Kevin Rock now in the leadership role of piloting the plot's creative direction a fresh set of eyes was needed for Rock's innovative Freak Show design. Richard Reams stepped up to the mark.

Reams, whose credits include *Buck Rogers in the 25th Century*, *Bonnie & Clyde: The True Story* and *Supernatural* gave the franchise, which was anything but assured, hope for the future, a look that helped the Direct-to-VHS stand out among its low-budget competitors – *Zombie Rampage*, *Children of the Night* and *Bad Karma*.

Here's Richard Reams' account of the transitioning franchise. He discusses his relationship with producers Steve Lane and Bob Pringle, the often-recreated but never-credited twisted clown mouth entrance and the phoney!

RICHARD REAMS

ON BEING *HOWLING VI: THE FREAKS*' PRODUCTION DESIGNER:

As the Production Designer, I was responsible for the overall look of the film. I personally hand-selected every person whose department might have a visual impact on the film. This included the Set Decorator, Simon Dobbin, costume designer and makeup artists ... including being involved in the selection of Todd Master and Steve Johnson, who did the Special Effects Make Up. I was brought on the project very early, with 2 months prep which was, and still is, a lot on a low budget film like this.

I was brought on by producers Steve Lane and Bob Pringle, whom I had known for many years as close friends. We all had roots in movie theatres and I even designed many movie theatres for them prior to this ... And prior to starting my career in production.

They approached me to help them prove that the film could be produced in Los Angeles, rather than taking it to Budapest. The money producers said there was no way it could be filmed in LA with a budget of a little over a million dollars.

I read the script and went back to Steve and Bob, and told them their money guy was right, that they couldn't make the film that was scripted for that kind of money, but I had a way to make it work.

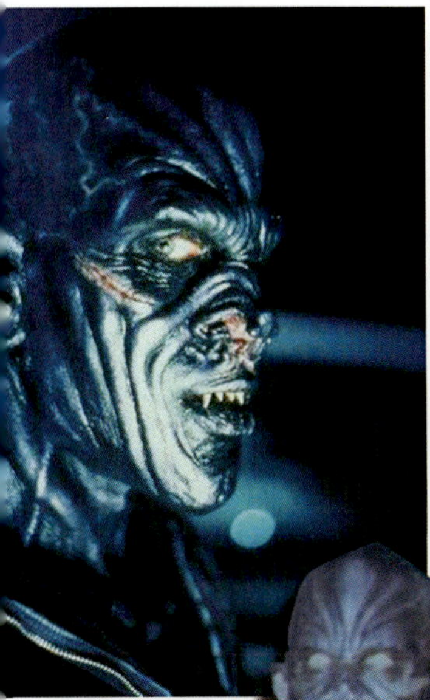

I spent several days with script writer Kevin Rock, and we went through the script and I told him what the set would be.

Basically, it would be taking all the scenes that had been written for a big carnival and midway and moving it all into a maze of interior sets, which is what you saw on the screen.

ON GOING FROM MIRAMAX'S *DIXIE LANES* TO *HOWLING VI: THE FREAKS*:

WOW ... OK ... totally different ... both were very low budget, but on *Howling* I had lots of prep and support from my friends.

I enjoyed *Dixie Lanes*, but it was really hard because I came in and replaced someone and had no prep at all ... hit the ground running with dressing sets to shoot the next day for most of the shoot ... fun cast .... Hoyt Axton, great guy ... And Tina Louise ... and the best was Ruth Buzzi ... So nice and so much fun.

ON HOW MUCH SAY HE HAD IN THE FINISHED LOOK OF *HOWLING VI: THE FREAKS'* PRODUCTION DESIGN:

Because of my relationship with Steve and Bob, I was given complete control and they just knew I would give them a great look with the money we had.

I had a really great Set Decorator, which was a huge help. I was very hands-on during filming, looking through the camera for almost every shot. There was only one scene that I was disappointed with.

ON HIS THOUGHTS ON THE PREVIOUS *HOWLING* MOVIES:

Being friends with Steve and Bob, I had seen all the prior films ... and I felt like I could bring something to the project, and that was my eye. I also felt it was one of the better ones and nothing better has come since then.

ON THE FILM'S SHOOTING SCHEDULE AND ITS PRODUCTION:

For me it was easy because I had a great crew who had my back and were friends who I had pulled in all my favours with ... but it was hard because I'm a bit of a perfectionist and this was my film as Production Designer. I was working for friends and wanted to do the very best.

The entire creative team were great together!

ON WHAT INSPIRED HIS PRODUCTION DESIGN:

I did so much research on old freak shows and carnivals ... wanted to give it a bit of the old world look ... didn't look at other films, just researched the old live side shows.

ON WORKING WITH HOPE PERELLO AND HER SKILL AS A DIRECTOR:

I truly loved working with Hope ... now at first she was a bit taken because I was hired weeks before her ... but if it wasn't for my making the budget doable in LA ... I don't know if she would have gotten the job.

She [Hope Perello], like all of us, made the best out of what we had to work with.

ON WORKING DIRECTLY WITH THE DIRECTOR, CINEMATOGRAPHER AND PRODUCER:

I had been a Set Decorator for many years and worked closely with all these departments before. [It was a] great experience and we had fun ... it was really a family atmosphere and we all worked well together.

ON WHAT HE FELT TURNED OUT VISUALLY THE BEST ON *HOWLING VI: THE FREAKS*:

The inside of the carnival and the sideshow ... Alligator boy was a lot of fun.

ON WHICH SCENE HE WAS GIVEN THE MOST ARTISTIC FREEDOM:

Just all the inside of the tent ... loved creating the twisted clown mouth entrance ... I had never seen that before, and I have since seen it copied in other movies.

ON HIS OVERALL FEELING OF *HOWLING VI: THE FREAKS*:

I was proud of our work ... I mean we had a very small budget and it looked like we spent three times more than we did.

ON WHETHER *HOWLING VI: THE FREAKS* STANDS UP TO TODAY'S YOUTUBE AUDIENCE:

I'm not sure ... I have not watched it in a long time ... but might need to...

ON WHAT HE WOULD GO BACK AND CHANGE IF HE HAD A TARDIS:

I would have not gone home sick one day. I was so sick, and that was the day I was disappointed with the moon outside the window where the Werewolf is changing ... you couldn't see it, but we built a miniature of orange groves outside the window and the moon was so bright and looked phoney and it burned out all the trees and hillside we had spent a long time building. ■

RELEASED
(USA, Oct 24, 1995)

DIRECTOR
Clive Turner,
Roger Nall

WRITING CREDITS
Gary Brandner
(*The Howling I, II & III*)

STORY
Clive Turner

SCREENPLAY
Clive Turner

CINEMATOGRAPHER
Andreas Kossak

COMPOSER
Guy Moon

CAST
John Ramsden (Detective),
Ernest Kester (Ernie),
Clive Turner (Ted Smith),
John Huff (Father John),
Cheryl Allen (Cheryl),
Claude 'Pappy' Allen (Pappy),
Romy Walthall (Marie Adams)

PRODUCTION COMPANY
Allied Vision,
Allied Entertainments Group PLC,
LIVE Entertainment

EDITOR
Clive Turner

SPECIAL EFFECTS
Jerry Macaluso

RUNNING TIME
90 min

Howling VII : New Moon Rising

Somewhere Out There a New Terror is Breeding

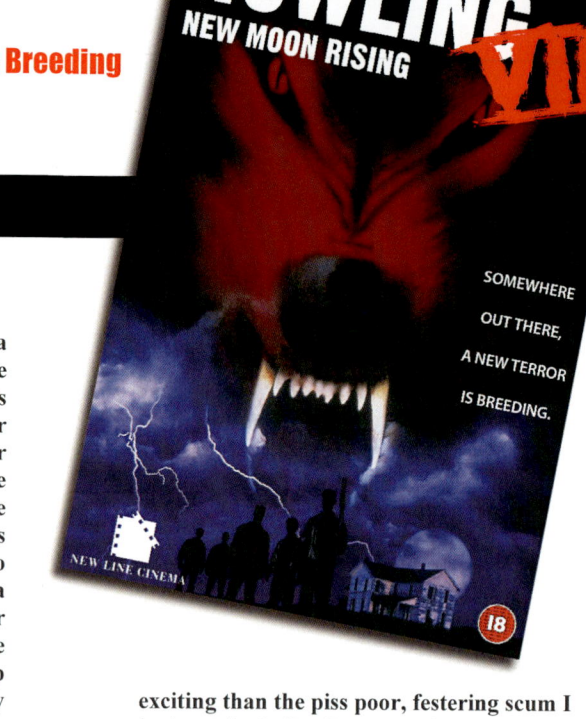

SYNOPSIS

An Australian man named Ted (Clive Turner), intricately connected to the previous three *Howling* films, arrives in a small western town where he begins to mingle with the local townsfolk, secretly recording his own enigmatic agendas into a tape recorder in his hotel room. At the same time a number of mysterious slayings appearing to be the work of a large animal begin to occur in the area. A detective (John Ramsden) investigates the case, helped by a priest (John Huff), who is certain the killings are the work of a werewolf, leading the two of them to uncover several clues that connect events from the previous three films in the series with the help of Marie Adams, an author tormented by what she witnessed in the small town of Drago that left her husband and friend dead!

"In fact... the above description is far more exciting than the piss poor, festering scum I just watched. Joe Dante would be spinning in his grave."

Hot Donkey Bear

The *Howling* was a brutal, electrifying tale of woman (Dee Wallace) meets beast, only to become the inner demon she conquered. *Howling II* was a tale of revenge and retribution, breast delight with gleeful camp overtones. *Howling III* told the story of how different tribes lived and hunted whilst becoming the hunted – sharing elements that some could compare to a docudrama broadcast on the Discovery channel but produced by Comedy Central. *Howling IV* was more or less a lowbrow franchise reboot, pulling out all the stops but failing at the last hurdle. *Howling V* held its head just long enough above the surface to survive its low budget juxtaposition to *The Beast Must Die*.

Howling VI was grafted loosely from Gary Brandner's third novel in the best-selling book trilogy and gave viewers a fresh approached to the popular lycanthropy stereotype, and *Howling VII* – well, here we go!

Howling VII: New Moon Rising was released in 1995 direct-to-video, and had to fight for rental shop shelf space alongside *Candyman: Farwell to Flesh* (Bill Nunn), *Species* (Forest Whitaker), *Halloween: The Curse of Michael Myers* (Paul Rudd), *Leprechaun 3* (Warwick Davis), *Texas Chainsaw: The Next Generation* (Renee Zellweger) and a remake of *Piranha* (Mila Kunis), to name just a few. So looking at the competition

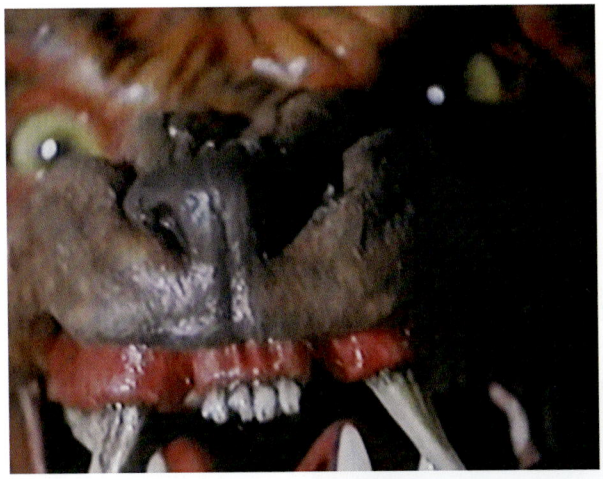

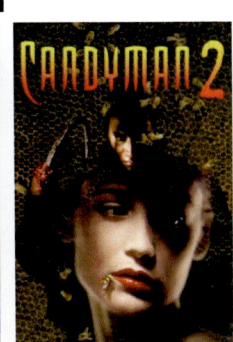

it was no real surprise that *Howling VII* wouldn't perform as successfully as earlier entries in the series when up against a title like Clive Barker's *Candyman: Farwell to Flesh*, so the decision by producers to cut back on the film's budget was a sound one and made good business sense. But other aspects of the film's production weren't so sound! And as TV Guide remarked upon the film's release, it was "a new low for the franchise", one which would force the brand's name into dormancy for 15 long years, but not long enough to erase *New Moon Rising* from audiences' minds.

Clive Turner came into the series in 1988 as a co-producer and writer on *The Howling: The Original Nightmare* (later re-shooting much of John Hough's footage), and went on to produce, write and star in *Howling V: The Rebirth*. Throughout his time spent with the franchise Turner, a frustrated director and actor (*Howling IV* and *V*), battled constantly for his own vision to be the more dominant presence in each film's running time. He took a hiatus from the series in 1992 to executively produce the $10m adaptation of Stephen King's *The Lawnmower Man* (Jeff Fahey), but returned to his hunting ground to supervise post-production on *VI* before directing, editing, writing, producing and starring in *The Howling VII*, a concept lazily patched together that follows an Australian man named Ted Smith (Clive Turner), who is intricately connected to the previous two *Howling* (*IV, V*) films.

Smith arrives in a small western town where he mingles with the local townsfolk, secretly recording his own enigmatic agendas into a tape recorder in the rundown squalor of his hotel room. At the same time a number of mysterious slayings within the area occur, all appearing to be the work of a large animal, or are they? A detective (Ernest Kester) investigates the case, helped by a priest, Father John (John Huff), who is certain that the killings are the work of "a demon, a werewolf". This leads the two unlikely wolfbusters, a half-sharp detective and a priest who specializes in bizarre phenomena, to uncover several clues that connect these fresh events to earlier proceedings in the franchise, cue ample stock footage.

Like the character Ted Smith, lifeless and boring, Clive Turner clearly had a personal agenda. He made the seventh outing his star vehicle to break into Hollywood via the backdoor, and, credit were credit's due, he most definitely took the saying "If at first you don't succeed try, try again" very literally, but despite his best efforts his ambition fell flat and only garnered one role after *Howling VII* as a bouncer in the $3.4m movie *The Apostate* (Dennis Hopper) and he never directed again.

New Moon Rising was shot in 1994 in Pioneertown, California, an unincorporated community in the Morongo Basin region by route 62. Not only is Pioneertown a surreal place of wonder, its history, much like the *Howling* series, does not follow a normal narrative. Built as a film set in the 1940s by Hollywood movie-makers, its main feature is a four-block-long Main Street (as opposed to America's

and stock footage galore for almost no discernible reason. Many involved eventually asked for their names to be removed from the film's credits due to the finished product falling into the realm of bad paracinematic nonsense that made little sense to anyone involved apart from its star, who was also its writer-director-producer-accountant. Of course, nobody at the time would admit to that as they had bills to pay back home, so they kept their heads down to pick up their pay cheque!

Guy Moon was responsible for the film's musical composition. His previous credits include *Creepozoids*, *The Imp* (*Sorority Babes In The Slimeball Bowl-O-Rama*), *The Addams Family* (TV series) and *The Fairly OddParents*.

Prior to *New Moon Rising*, Moon provided the music for the $1m *The Brady Bunch Movie*, which took a whopping $47m at the box office, so cashing his cheque for *New Moon Rising* must have been bitter-sweet for the 4-times Primetime Emmy nominated musician.

Moon isn't the only guilty party in charge of music. The film includes four extended scenes of line dancing and approximately 12 country music montages performed by Claude 'Pappy' Allen, who passed away before he got to see the finished film. When Pappy Allen died, hundreds of mourners from around the world attended his memorial, including Victoria Williams, who later recorded the song *Happy to Have Known Pappy* for her Atlantic Records release on the album *Loose*. Much like *New Moon Rising*, *Happy to Have Known Pappy* was a commercial bomb along with the album, which failed miserably to make a dent on the Billboard Top 200.

Andreas Kossak was in charge of cinematography. He was one of the first people hired, he never got fired, he never quit, and he even sat in the editing room to the bitter end. He made a name for himself in the industry with Brett Thompson's 1991 *Adventures in Dinosaur City*, which did fairly well on VHS and was released by Republic Pictures, who distributed *Beverly Hills, 90210*. Unlike *New Moon Rising*, *Adventures in Dinosaur City* had a reasonable budget and has since gone on to gain cult status.

Helen Harwell, who also goes by the name Helen Harwell-Lewis, served as Art Director. Harwell was in charge of the overall visual appearance and how the film communicated visually with its target audience. In the same year that she worked on *New Moon Rising*, she also put her mark on the Dee Wallace feature film directed by Andrew Stevens, *The Skateboard Kid 2*. The shoot for *New Moon Rising* was probably the least complicated of the franchise, so it's hard to even understand how such a talented artist struggled so much to put her signature on the finished film. Since *New Moon Rising* Harwell has continued to work steadily and was the art director on *The Dentist 2*, *The Stepdaughter*, *The Courier* and the production designer on *The Pact II* and *5th of July*.

The position of make-up artist fell into the hands of 7-times Primetime Emmy nominated Stephanie A. Fowler. Fowler started out in the 1980s as a location scout before becoming an assistant makeup artist and then moving up to key makeup artist on *Project: Metalbeast* in 1995. Her work on *New Moon Rising* was minimal and it's hard to see what she actually did or was involved in.

John Huff was also very frail and had leukemia and was expected to only live for a few more weeks when filming began. Huff's scenes were all shot at night at the local two-room western church, and the crew were warned prior to Huff's arrival to make sure all setups were done quickly so Huff could shoot his scenes and leave.

Sound mixing was given to Charles Kelly (*Terminator: The Sarah Connor Chronicles*), who had impressed Turner on *Howling VI: The Freaks*. Kelly's credits within the genre were limited but he worked on the production sound of *Sorority House Massacre* and *Return to Horror High* before providing second unit on *Shocker*. Kelly, who goes by various names, is predominately known for his work in the 90s with *Playboy* and the late Anna Nicole Smith.

Allied Entertainment Group was the returning production company, with Kent Adamson, Harvey Goldsmith and Edward

  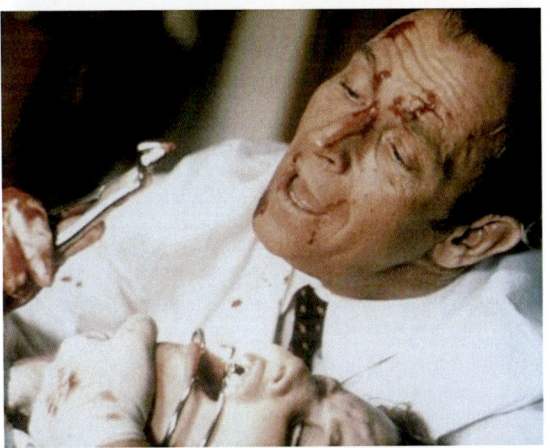 

Simons. Goldsmith and the other producers offered little in the way of artistic steering of the ship across the various films but still continued to receive credit and pick up their pay cheques.

New Moon Rising was finally released in the USA on October 24th 1995 in the run up to Halloween, and was distributed by New Line Cinema with little to no marketing.

In the UK the film was distributed by Park Entertainment and received the same treatment, but it was released under the name *The Howling VII: Mystery Woman*.

The critical reception for *New Moon Rising* wasn't pleasant. Almost every media outlet took a swipe at the film with Dread Central leading the angry mob, panning the film and warning viewers it would "eat" them "alive and without mercy."

Less than week in, video rental figures for the film came back and did nothing to silence the critics. Many VHS stores took the decision to cut their losses and put the VHS tape in the pre-used sales bin. The film was a financial and critical flop and no New Line logo at the start of the film or fan lip service could help.

In June 1999 Allied Home Entertainment released *Mystery Woman* on DVD to recoup their money. It was later released by Prism Leisure on the 10th October 2005 with the opening ten minutes featuring several brief audio dropouts. Marketing Film followed suit with a later release on DVD for its German audience, with various extras that included the film's original trailer, a photo gallery, cast and crew filmographies and bonus trailers, but it was quickly made unavailable due to lacklustre sales.

As the years went by the dust finally began to settle and much of the anger towards the film softened. Many *Howling* fans forgave Turner for knitting an un-cohesive narrative together in a quaint mid-90s country-and-western setting with very little werewolf action, eventually leading to a French Region 2 DVD release.

Nuits De Pleine Lune is by far the best version released to date, with an aspect ratio of 4:3 - 1.33:1, running at 90 minutes, full screen but it comes in dubbed French soundtrack format only. *New Moon Rising* has since popped up several times over the years on iOffer in the region free version from Dark Vision Collection simply titled *Howling 7* and billed as a rare collectable, uncut and fully restored edition.

Almost every media outlet took a swipe at the film with Dread Central leading the angry mob, panning the film and warning viewers it would "eat" them "alive and without mercy."

Suffice to say, due to the film's dismal reception, critical mauling and poor VHS rental/sales upon its original release, American distributors have since stayed well clear of the film. To date *New Moon Rising* has never received a DVD release in its place of conception but that's not to say it hasn't left its mark. Sadly, it's not the type of mark anyone ever wants to leave behind – R.I.P. *New Moon Rising*. ■

RELEASED
(USA, Oct 3, 2011)

DIRECTOR
Joe Nimziki

WRITING CREDITS
Gary Brandner
(*The Howling I, II & III*)

STORY
Joe Nimziki

SCREENPLAY
Joe Nimziki,
James Robert Johnston

CINEMATOGRAPHER
Benoit Beaulieu

COMPOSER
Christopher Carmichael,
Mark Yaeger

CAST
Landon Liboiron (Will Kidman),
Lindsey Shaw (Eliana Wynter),
Ivana Milicevic (Kathryn),
Jesse Rath (Sachin),
Kristian Hodko (Tribe)

PRODUCTION COMPANY
Anchor Bay Films,
Moonstone Entertainment

EDITOR
James Coblentz,
Joe Nimziki

SPECIAL EFFECTS
Marc Auclair,
Louis Craig,
Karim El Fassi,
Bernard Guay
Sebastien Roussel,
Sandra Solanchick,
Luc Therrien

RUNNING TIME
Israel, 79 min,
Turkey, 87 min,
USA, 88 min

The Howling: Reborn
Full Moon. New Blood.

SYNOPSIS

In the Shermer High School the teenager Will Kidman (Landon Liboiron) is bullied by his school mate Roland. Will lost his mother (Ivana Milicevic) when he was born and he lives alone with his father, Jack Kidman (Frank Schorpion). Will's best friend (Jesse Rath) is the aspirant horror film director Sachin and he dreams of his mysterious school mate Eliana Wynter (Lindsey Shaw), for whom he has yearned for a long time. On his eighteenth birthday and eve of his graduation day, Will is invited to go to an underground party and he stays with Eliana. Will is drugged by a colleague and he has the sensation that a werewolf attacked people in the party. Out of the blue Will gets stronger and stronger and he suspects that he might be a werewolf. When the evil Kay meets Will at school he learns dark secrets about his past and finds

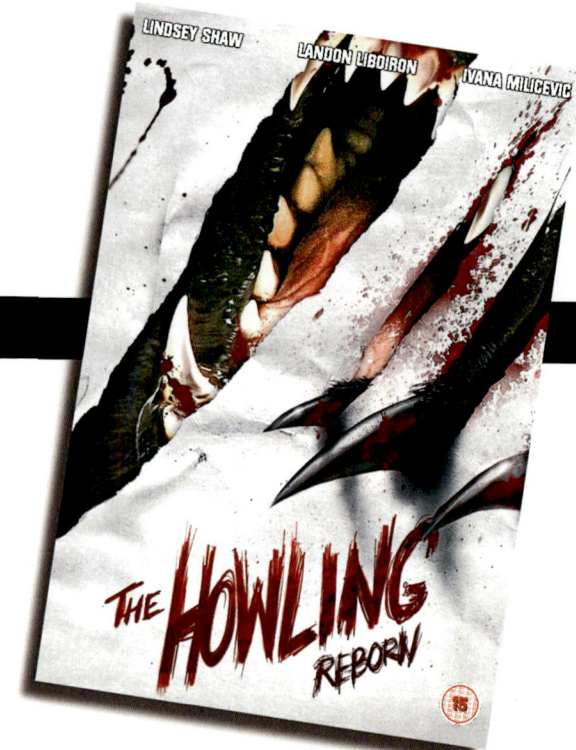

that Eliana might be in danger.

The Howling: Reborn promised to be a return to form for the franchise and after the dreaded and almost impossible to watch *Howling VII: New Moon Rising*, directed by series veteran Clive Turner, who on previous movies doubled as editor, writer, interferer and on-set drug dealer. "He was the on-set drug dealer among other things," stated Bull Forsche (Bill Forsche) when discussing his former boss. *The Howling: Reborn* looked like it could at least achieve the goal of being better than its predecessor if all else failed.

The Howling: Reborn was written and directed by Joe Nimziki. Nimziki became involved in the production after the project's producer, Joel Kastleberg (*Sleep with Me*), had purchased the rights to the film's title with the intention of making a feature film that would then transition from the big screen to the small (episodic TV show). "I was approached (and I was interested) to do

"We did a lot of auditions, Los Angeles, Vancouver, Toronto, Montreal, New York, on and on, so we saw a lot of kids. And even more by tape and by Internet and by various other means. We whittled down the candidates and brought people back and back and Landon was the last one standing."

something new. I was a fan of the original and my thought was, some 30 years later, we could take the story in a younger and more personal direction (with great creatures and a dash of social commentary like the original) and hopefully make a worthy successor," stated Nimziki on becoming involved in the *Howling VIII* (working title), which would later become *Reborn*.

Nimziki began writing the film almost immediately alongside James Robert Johnston (*Joy Ride 2: Dead Ahead*). Nimziki invested a lot of himself into the film's characters and once the script was complete the arduous task of casting began.

Rosina Bucci and Vera Miller were brought on board but Nimziki oversaw almost every aspect of the process. Bucci and Miller were both established casting directors within their sector and Bucci had among her credits *Being Human*, *Big Wolf on Campus* and *Scanners II: The New Order*. While *The New Order* was more notable for a few undeniably bad turns from its bit parts Bucci's résumé is otherwise immaculate. Miller's work, while more oriented to the TV movie genre, cast for some notable movies of the week, *Deadly Isolation* and *Deadly Betrayal*.

Nimziki stated in regards to the role of Will Kidman, "We did a lot of auditions, Los Angeles, Vancouver, Toronto, Montreal, New York, on and on, so we saw a lot of kids. And even more by tape and by Internet and by various other means. We whittled down the candidates and brought people back and back and Landon was the last one standing."

Landon Liboiron, who sports the Harry Potter vibe throughout the movie, later went onto star in *Hemlock Grove* but was better known prior to *The Howling: Reborn* for a recurring role in *Degrassi: The Next Generation*. The role of his on-screen love interest, Eliana Wynter, went to Lindsey Shaw, while that of his best friend, Sachin, went to Jesse Rath from Montreal and the role of lead villain and matriarch to Ivana Milicevic. "I had known Joe for a while

because I had met him before," Milicevic stated. "He was familiar with my work when I met him for this movie. I just really liked him, I really wanted to work with him and I liked that he wanted control and wanted to pick the people he wanted to see in these parts."

Filming took place in Canada in May 2010 and originally Nimziki was adamant he wanted to have Dee Wallace return to reprise her role from the first film. But the producers put the kibosh on that idea due to having to pay for the character actress's air fare and accommodation in addition to hiring her to perform. "I had written a small part for Dee Wallace, who wanted to come up for a few days and shoot it, and the request was refused because a producer didn't want to pay for her flight to Canada," the director said, voicing his dismay. "Dee would have been great and we could have tipped our hat to the original. As a former studio exec, it was obvious to me that the $1,500 to fly her out would've returned itself many times over in publicity."

The Executives not only made the decision not to have Wallace's involvement but prior to filming the studio also demanded *The Howling: Reborn* to be shot as PG 13 to broaden its appeal. "Right before production I was told I had to quickly change my scary, R rated love story to a soft PG 13 love story. This was something I really didn't want to do. I lobbied to be able to at least shoot it both ways so they would either be able to see they were wrong or at the least there could be a new cut for digital, but I was told 'No'," Nimziki said.

But PG 13 aside Nimziki pressed on and *The Howling: Reborn* not only reintroduced 'The' into the brand name but the FX team reintroduced Rob Bottin's original designs, making sure they added their own original twist into the aesthetic. Marc Auclair (*The Mummy*), Louis Craig (*The Fly*), Karim El Fassi (*Death Race*), Bernard Guay (*Big Wolf on Campus*), Sebastien Roussel (*Rabid Dogs*), Sandra Solanchick (*Hollywood Wasteland*) and Luc Therrien (*Riddick*) dealt with bringing the monsters to life on a budget that had been slashed in half by the time they were hired.

"We wanted to come with a new werewolf, which is not easy because it has been drawn for the past 2000 years," said Yuda Acco (*Power Rangers Turbo*). Acco delt with *Reborn*'s production design, a task that had previously gone to Richard Reams on *Howling VI: The Freaks*. "If you put the wolf into Google you're going to get about 2000 pages."

The Howling: Reborn used foam latex when creating their creatures due to it being resilient and very soft, and the creature's teeth were created from modified composite resins that are used in the process of making dentures. Nimziki said of the design, "On an aesthetic level we were hoping we could go back old-school with the werewolves."

Besides the foam latex werewolves the team behind the magic used several animatronic heads. The creatures had numerous switches beneath there facial skin, which was approximately an eighth of an inch of foam with a fibreglass armature underneath, which was cut into different sections of the face. Every section could be made to move by using remote control servos, the same servo motors that are used in remote control aircraft. There were over 20 servos in each of the werewolf heads, which made the suits extremely heavy to wear for long periods of time.

The Howling: Reborn was shot in just 20 days. It was originally scheduled for 70 days but once again, like with every other *Howling* movie, the powers-that-be cut corners by reducing budget and time. They shipped the production to Montreal for financial reasons. "We were working with a much depleted crew. We came to Montreal so last minute that summer, and there were seven big films already shooting, so finding everyone from a DP to PA's was beyond difficult."

Due to the film's relocation Nimziki found it incredibly hard to fill the entire crew, so many of them had to double up in several roles. "I am very satisfied with what [we] pulled off with the days, money, crew and various issues we did have," Nimziki added, and this was seconded by his loyal and hardworking cast. "Joe is crazy! He's been in the business for a really long time so it's really cool to see how much he understands what a set should be," said Liboiron. "It's [was] a pretty ambitious project; we [were] doing a film in 25 days, where it should probably [have been] 50 or 70 days. Joe knows exactly what he wants and we just [had] to do the work." Shaw, who went onto star in *Pretty Little Liars*, stated, "To be directed by Joe is wonderful, he has a constant smile on his face and [even] if things [were] going a little slow or behind schedule..."

The Howling: Reborn suffered immensely in its pre-media build up due to the associations made with *Twilight*, which overshadowed many aspects of the film, and upon the film's delivery the studio executives once again changed their minds about what they wanted, even after its first round of marketing which highlighted the film's PG 13 rating. Months prior to the movie's release they now decided they wanted to marketed *Reborn* as an R. "This process of shooting the film PG 13 and releasing it as a bloody horror R was particularly frustrating to me," said the director disappointedly, "having been the head creative and marketing executive at several major studios before making the switch to writing and directing. I had to witness these mis-steps of judgment and

strategy and material, knowing where we were headed as a result, but was ultimately powerless to do anything about it."

The Howling: Reborn was released on October 18, 2011 and horror media outlets wasted no time in pulling the film apart limb by limb. "Jesus, after *New Moon Rising* I didn't think the series could go any lower!" stated Horror Geek. Horror News wrote, ""H8" gets ½ a shroud from The Black Saint for some of its performances but that's it. It's not worth the price of a rental from a Redbox machine ($1.00). Avoid at all costs unless you're a completist, and even if you are, walk past it." Arrow in the Head stated, "Far too tethered to the PG-13 sensibilities of TWILIGHT and its ilk, too predictable (dialogue and story), and even with its descriptions of graphic gore, shows very little bite. At the end of the day, REBORN is a non-scary, teen-centric missed opportunity!" and Dread Central remarked that *The Howling: Reborn* was more of "a failed CW pilot

than R-rated sequel, it can't be bothered with any effort to scare its audience or entertain through sheer exploitation or gleeful gore."

Not only did the film come under criticism from Dread Central but Anchor Bay's bargain bin approach to the film's Blu-ray release did too. "Anchor Bay brings *The Howling: Reborn* to Blu-ray in a mediocre high definition transfer, the worst offender of rampant banding I've seen in some time (just look at that scene where a werewolf drops through the ceiling and lands on a table – yikes). Color saturation is fine (it's a drab-looking film to begin with), but detail isn't always prevalent. The image is often flat, and textures can be nonexistent depending on the shot."

Since its initial DVD release in the USA a number of European territories got to see *The Howling: Reborn* in 3D, which included a theatrical release in Turkey on April 13, 2012. The film's UK release was less fortunate, released April, 9th 2012 with cover art that resembled Cujo shredding his way through bed sheets on a washing line. The film was rated 15 by the BBFC and the uninspired box art accompanying the film got lost among the DVDs on the shelves. Starz Inc., a subsidiary of Anchor Bay Entertainment, even reduced its marketing budget, stripping spend right back, and they even bypassed sending screeners out to journalists. Germany, who additionally got a 3D cut of the film, dropped *The Howling* from its title and settled on *BlueMoon*, with artwork inspired by *Twilight* and *Harry Potter* – an agenda to try and avoid its association with

the previously posted negative reviews.

The film's timing and interference from the production company saw *The Howling: Reborn* die a slow DVD death. With video rental shops being a thing of the past the film struggled to find an audience, and while it did eventually find a minuscule fan base it wasn't big enough to warrant a follow-up movie or a *Buffy The Vampire Slayer* inspired TV show. The studio killed the continued discussion with Nimziki, leaving him with a completed pilot show script all dressed up with nowhere to go.

With *The Howling IX* nixed the brand name wasn't. Emaji Entertainment and Front Row Filmed Entertainment optioned *The Howling* title in 2016. Gianluca Chakra (*StrangeLand*) and Robert Atwell (*StrangeLand*), the film's producers, have set their sights on retooling the series. Whether the production will churn out another unrelated sequel or reboot from the series source material is not known but what is, is that you can't keep a good werewolf down, here's to *The Howling*.... ■

8.

The Joe Nimziki interview

The series spawned by Joe Dante's classic 1981 werewolf outing was resurrected by Moonstone Entertainment, helmed and scripted by Joe Nimziki. *The Howling: Reborn* came with varied critical brushstrokes and was immediately pigeonholed as a *Twilight* afterthought when dropped amongst the teen-aimed horror thrills of 2011 without any pre-build-up.

Scream 4 (Neve Campbell), *Red Riding Hood* (Amanda Seyfried), *Beastly* (Vanessa Hudgens), *Abduction* (Taylor Lautner) and *Final Destination 5* (Emma Bell) all came backed by star power, while Joe Nimziki's *The Howling: Reborn* had to rely on word-of-mouth purchase and horror fans ignoring the film's online critical reception and *Twilight* comparisons.

Had *The Howling: Reborn* been dropped a decade earlier, pre-*Twilight* with a bigger budget, Joe Nimziki would no doubt have been hailed for his part in reinvigorating the teen horror genre as a result of *The Howling: Reborn*'s smart, sarcastic, self-aware script. Nimziki's way with hyper-articulate, wise-beyond-their-years teen characters would certainly have made him an object of desire, much like screenwriter Kevin Williamson.

The Howling: Reborn reboot vehicle was a teen-centric, sensitive, emotionally-driven drama with werewolves all marooned in a near future high school setting. Nimziki portrayed his teens as smart, capable young adults with intense self-reflection, allowing them to talk in long, considered, usually perfectly constructed sentences and, just like his central characters, Joe Nimziki has come prepared to battle against *The Howling: Reborn* haters and tell his side of the story.

JOE NIMZIKI

ON THE ATTRACTION OF WRITING AND DIRECTING *THE HOWLING: REBORN*:

I was always interested in werewolves as a mythology and as a metaphor. The original *Howling* definitely made an impression on me as a kid and still deserves a lot of credit to this day for the leap forward it represented in the depiction of the creatures on film.

THE BIRTH OF *THE HOWLING: REBORN*:

I was approached to write and direct by producer Joel Kastleberg, who had just purchased the rights. I'd just had a film I was attached to fall through at MGM and was available.

RESERVATIONS AND CONCERNS ABOUT TAKING ON A WELL-KNOWN FILM SERIES:

Obviously there are a lot of true fans of the original (and deservedly so). And I've never really seen the need for a lot of the remakes Hollywood does (they often feel like simple cash grabs). On the other hand, a lot of time had passed since the original. I hadn't (and still haven't) seen any of the sequels. And I was approached to do something different and try to set a new course for the franchise, which appealed to me.

THE HOWLING: REBORN PIGGYBACKING OFF THE *TWILIGHT* CRAZE:

Our film was delayed, fell apart and was

resurrected so many times over the years that by the time we actually filmed the *Twilight* book had been written and the film released. Of course, I was disappointed that we would come out after and possibly be seen as derivative as a result, but the producers and studio all loved the script as it was and were determined to move forward. And though, like *Twilight*, we were bringing our genre into the world of high school, my intention was always to do a very scary and R rated love story that would still set us apart to some extent.

THE HOWLING: REBORN'S TERRIBLE RELEASE STRATEGY:

When I signed on *The Howling: Reborn* was conceived and developed to be a much bigger studio release. But due to bankruptcies, sales, etc. we ended up with Starz and Anchor Bay and literally a tiny fraction ($2 million) of the original budget ($20 million). Of course, that was still okay as we finally had a chance to shoot our movie, which is always a good thing. But then, right before production, I was told I had to quickly change my scary, R rated love story to a soft PG 13 love story. This was something I really didn't want to do. I lobbied to be able to at least shoot it both ways (so they would either be able to see they were wrong or at the least there could be a new cut for digital but I was told "no").

As a result, I ended up cutting a bunch of fun and important scenes and moments to conform to their request. But the real issue was after we delivered our finished film, the studio decided that despite their earlier mandate it should now be marketed as an R rated (and Non-Rated digital and DVD) film. That obviously wasn't the film we had and it really created a worst of both worlds scenario where the initial movie-goers who wanted to see that scary R rated film were surely going to be disappointed.

This process of shooting the film PG 13 and releasing it as a bloody horror R was particularly frustrating to me having been the head creative and marketing executive at several major studios before making the switch to writing and directing. I had to witness these mis-steps of judgement and strategy and material, knowing where we were headed as a result, but was ultimately powerless to do anything about it.

The good news is that movies live on long after an initial release. And as time has passed, and the right audience has found it, the reception of the film has been wonderful. I hear that high school kids quote it to each other. And I can't tell you how many meetings I go to for my current projects where the execs or assistants tell me they saw it on HBO or Netflix or whatever and really enjoyed it. I still am upset that we didn't make the scarier R rated love story we set out to… but that said I'm glad that the audience for the film we did make eventually found the film after the misguided marketing and initial release.

Oh, and we initially conceived doing the film in 3D as well… so it was interesting to see some territories in Europe re-released *The Howling: Reborn* in 3D.

ON THE HOWLING: REBORN'S PRODUCER, ROBERT PRINGLE (HOWLING II, III, IV, V, VI):

I never met him. I was approached (and I

was interested) to do something new. I was a fan of the original and my thought was, some 30 years later, we could take the story in a younger and more personal direction (with great creatures and a dash of social commentary like the original) and hopefully make a worthy Successor.

ON THE *THE HOWLING: REBORN*'S PROBLEMS VS JOHN HOUGH'S DEVASTATING ON-SET TREATMENT AND THE RESHOOT OF ALMOST 70% OF *HOWLING IV: THE ORIGINAL NIGHTMARE*:

For the most part during filming and post it was the previously mentioned issues. Of course, there were countless other problems, like all films, that were relatively minor in the scheme of things. But no coups or reshoots or anything like that. For instance, I had a strong vision for the score and soundtrack (I always do as music is so important to me). In the end the composer Klaus Badelt loved the project and signed on for almost nothing compared to what he normally gets to do the score. And all of the great recording artists we used in the film saw a rough cut of the film and contributed their songs for next to nothing. But there was one song that I was forced to cut (which really took the opening titles to another level) and another that was forced to be replaced by a producer (and I cringe every time I'm flipping around on TV and see the scene where Will meets Kathryn for the first time after school as a result). But compared to what it sounds like John went through… nothing that bad.

THE IMPORTANCE OF A DIRECTOR PROTECTING HIS OEUVRE:

I think it is important to fight the good fight. On *Reborn*, for instance, I could see the mis-steps that were being made regarding tone and release wearing both my hat as a filmmaker and my hat as an executive, which made it doubly difficult. As hard as it was to have these decisions made, it would have been worse knowing I didn't fight them as hard as possible.

ON *THE HOWLING: REBORN* PUSHING THE WEREWOLF ENVELOPE IN THE DIALOGUE AND NARRATIVE DEPARTMENT:

I feel like a lot of the dialogue is the one thing that remained largely intact through all the budget cuts, scheduling cuts, and ill-conceived distributor decisions. I enjoy hearing that high school students now quote the film to each other. Of course, I think the dialogue and characters would have stood out more as a kind of counterpoint to the original visceral version of the story. But I'm glad you and others have responded to it so well.

I also get a lot of nice comments about Will's voice-over throughout the film… though I actually wrote all of that in the edit bay out of necessity as a band aid of sorts. A way to clarify and unify the story after scenes were cut and tone was shifted just before principal photography.

I think the fact that what remains of the characters and dialogue has seemed to strike a chord with folks is the primary reason I've been approached several times to turn the feature into a TV series.

ON THE POSSIBILITY *THE HOWLING : REBORN* WAS MADE HARDER TO MARKET DUE TO ITS *DAWSON CREEK* MEETS *TEEN WOLF* ELEMENTS AND ITS UNWORLDLY, IDEALISTIC CHARM, A TEEN ROMANCE WITH TEETH AND CLAWS:

I'd actually like to believe (even if I'm wrong) that it was the opposite case. The studio sold it as more of the same when I think the audience would have liked a "teen romance with teeth and claws" as you put it. The way the film has gained an audience and momentum since its initial release is, I believe, a testament to that. I think had the producers and studio backed sticking to the original vision of an R rated horror romance and sold it as such we'd be having a different discussion now.

I believe the more visceral, scary and emotional love story would have felt fresh and interesting and an audience would have come. If I didn't believe that, I obviously never would have signed on or written the original screenplay that way. And I think the small budget we suddenly

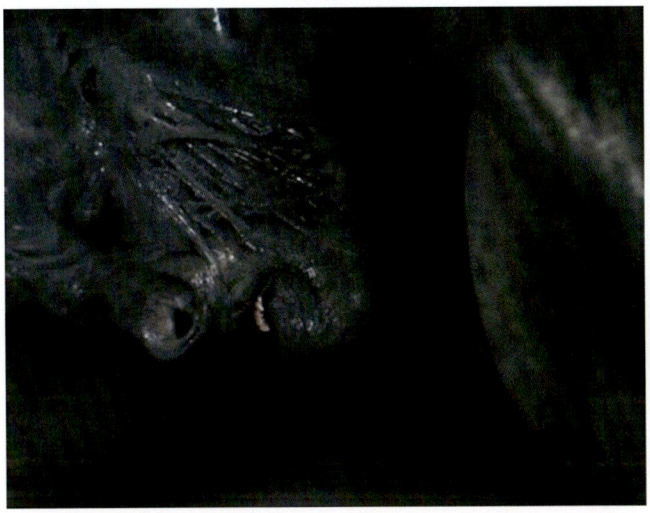

> "My single biggest regret to this day was I had written a small part for Dee Wallace (star of the original) who wanted to come up for a few days and shoot it and the request was refused because a producer didn't want to pay for her flight to Canada."

had at the end made it even more imperative to do something and take a fresh route (because we could never equal the production values of a *Twilight* or *Harry Potter* or whatever PG 13 fare we would be compared to).

HIGH EXPECTATIONS AND CONCERNS THE FILM WOULD UNDER-DELIVER:

At our initial budget we were going to do, I believe, awesome things worthy of the original. Through working on various genre pictures through the years as an executive with the likes of designers like HR Giger (*Alien*) and the top VFX houses like WETA (*Lord of the Rings*) I had put together an amazing team and we were going to do a lot of exciting and very original things with the creatures.

Of course, when we ended up months later on a mini budget in Montreal, that all changed. On top of that the local Montreal company we ended up with had so many delays making and delivering the creatures (in fairness to them some of these delays were due to them not being paid on time). We didn't even get any werewolf costumes until very late into the shooting schedule and had to cut scenes with them as a result. It was actually ultimately fortunate that we somehow shot all that we did before we wrapped. And when all was said and done, considering the money and time we had to do the creature scenes we still could, they turned out as well as anyone could have hoped.

THE IMPORTANCE OF PRACTICAL WEREWOLF EFFECTS:

Since our film was in essence a love story, the hope (even when we initially set to go at the big budget) was to make everything feel as real as possible. It was also a way we could pay homage to the original (as in its time it set a standard for realistic werewolf costumes and practical effects).

PRACTICAL EFFECTS BEING MORE UNFEASIBLE TO SHOOT DUE TO TIME AND BUDGET CONSTRAINTS:

Yes, that is often the case. But in our case we stuck to the plan in preproduction (obviously not anticipating the delays with the costumes) because in addition to the aesthetic we were going for we believed we could control the camera and movement and blocking and performance of the creatures better than the VFX folks we had could do afterward.

ON CASTING *THE HOWLING: REBORN*:

We were lucky that for our genre and for our budget we had some very talented folks interested in our film because they connected with the screenplay. We were also unlucky to lose some amazing actors because they were literally just a few dollars more expensive than others (money I would have gladly found elsewhere). But in the end, I was really happy with the three leads we cast in LA (Lindsey, Ivana and Landon). Montreal was another story as it was a struggle to find actors for the rest of the parts (partly due to the fact that the great ones were busy on one of the many other productions already happening when we arrived).

ON CASTING DEE WALLACE:

My single biggest regret to this day was I had written a small part for Dee Wallace (star of the original) who wanted to come up for a few days and shoot it and the request was refused because a producer didn't want to pay for her flight to Canada. Again, these types of decisions were hard for me on multiple levels. As a director, Dee would have been great and we could have tipped our hat to the original. As a former studio exec, it was obvious to me that the $1,500 to fly her out would've returned itself many times over in publicity and street cred to the fans of the original.

I know a lot of writers picture actors as they write, but usually I don't. I like to stay open to the process. I thought Landon was a nice mix awkward/handsome and boy/man that was a good fit for the role. When Lindsey's reps said she'd like to come in for Eliana I was happy because I was a fan. We could have gone a lot of different ways with Kathryn but I thought Milla was a near perfect fit.

Despite having some great options in LA I was ultimately forced to cast Sachin locally in Montreal. I saw so many kids but nobody was right. I can't tell you how relieved I was when, right before we started shooting, Jesse walked in to audition. He was great.

ACTORS CONSIDERED FOR ROLES IN *THE HOWLING: REBORN*:

We had great actors who wanted to be involved, all willing to work for scale. But due to scheduling, or more often a few thousand bucks more in accompanying expenses associated with them (hair/make-up/travel), I was not allowed to cast them. The father, for instance, is a role I cut down in the film you see because I couldn't cast several way-too-good-for-our-little-genre-film actors who wanted the role because of the bit of extra money involved.

ON LANDON LIBOIRON (WILL KIDMAN):

Landon was definitely the biggest risk I took in casting but, like you, I think he was great. He had never carried a film or played this type of character arc before, so he definitely felt some pressure. And I definitely had to work with him in a different way than the other actors (but this is almost always the case with an ensemble). But I think Landon dug down, committed and gave a really good performance.

THE HOWLING: REBORN'S FILMING SCHEDULE:

Way too fast! Just 20 days of shooting for a film originally scheduled for 70! And almost no second unit for a film that was originally supposed to have it every day. On top of that, we were working with a much depleted crew. We came to Montreal so last minute that summer, and there were seven big films already shooting, so finding everyone from a DP to PA's was beyond difficult. We never filled out the entire crew and lost a few more folks along the way. So, though it's tempting to think about what could have been with the original vision and budget and schedule of *Reborn*... I am also very satisfied with what pulled off with the days, money, crew and various issues we did have.

ON *THE HOWLING: REBORN* HIGHLIGHTS:

I think what I remember most fondly is shooting the handful of scenes that remained largely intact from the original screenplay I'd written. The primarily talking relationship scenes remained, for the most part, what they are. I think I

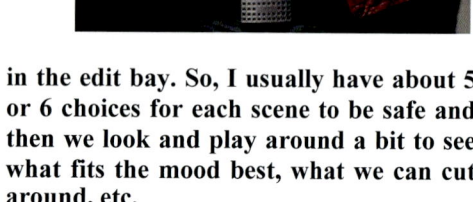

most enjoyed bringing to life those scenes between Will and Eliana and Sachin… the first kiss, the library, making weapons, broadcasting their warning, etc.

THE HOWLING: REBORN AFTER-HOURS FUN:

Sleep. We were on such a tight schedule. Though Saturday nights were fun (as we were off Sundays). Usually Lindsey, Landon, Milla and I would all act like the tourists we were and head out to dinner or a movie or a bar together. Montreal is such a great city and we were shooting in the summer during Jazzfest, so we definitely tried to squeeze in a little fun time when we could.

THE HOWLING: REBORN'S FLUID FILMING AND THE DEVELOPMENT OF THE LOVE TRIANGLE BETWEEN THE TWO LEADS:

For 20 days, no second unit and a largely inexperienced crew, I'm really happy with the amount and quality of the footage we did get. And I think Lindsey really helped ground the love triangle with her performance. Knowing the crazy schedule we were on, she came ready to nail it on take one or two every time. I can't say enough about her.

THE IMPORTANCE OF A FILM'S SCORE:

Music is very important to me. The songs you hear are largely the songs I wrote the script to. As I said earlier, there are a couple of areas where, despite being offered the songs for next to nothing, I wasn't allowed to use them and those scenes suffer as a result. But overall, I like how the music complements the film and I get so many people asking me where they can buy the soundtrack (which, unfortunately, was never released).

ON SELECTING THE HOWLING REBORN'S MUSIC TO MATCH A SCENE:

I wrote to a lot of it. I also played it on the set as we prepared to shoot each scene. But in the end, you never really know what music works or doesn't until you line it up with the picture in the edit bay. So, I usually have about 5 or 6 choices for each scene to be safe and then we look and play around a bit to see what fits the mood best, what we can cut around, etc.

ON THE FILM'S EDITING PROCESS:

I had final cut in my deal. I was on a very short post production schedule, but because of the quick shoot and scenes that had to be cut last minute I knew editing would be paramount to making sure the story at least made sense. I brought in Jim Clobentz to edit, who I worked with on *Final Destination* when I was at New Line. We had to do an assembly, incorporate VFX and music, and finalize a cut in 10 weeks. So, we set up an edit bay next door to my office in Manhattan Beach and worked tirelessly until time was up.

It's funny because I am often hired to come in and fix (via writing, directing and editing) troubled films, and because of my objectivity on those projects, it's very easy for me to see what's wrong and how we can fix things. But when you've written and directed something you lose that objectivity in the edit bay. You're remembering the scene before you had to cut it for budget, or the performance that you wanted but didn't have time to nail due to the tight schedule. I definitely wish we had a little more time in editing because we were still making the film better every day when the plug was pulled. When I see the film on TV now I see pacing issues and some other stuff that drives me a little crazy. But again, all said, I'm pretty proud of what we ended up delivering under the circumstances.

THE HOWLING: REBORN PROPERTY AND ITS POTENTIAL TELEVISION SERIES:

I wrote a pilot.

I've been approached several times since the release.

Usually a studio or network exec sees the film on HBO or Netflix and calls me in wanting to develop it into a show. I obviously love the franchise and the characters we created within it... but ultimately, there are rights issues involved and I just couldn't sign up to work with the same folks I did the film with for some of the reasons cited above (and many more not cited).

ON EMAJI ENTERTAINMENT AND FRONT ROW FILMED ENTERTAINMENT'S *THE HOWLING* REBOOT:

I think there will always be interest for a good *Howling* movie. I wish them all the best.

ON RETURNING TO *THE HOWLING* FRANCHISE FOR ONE MORE MOVIE:

Probably not. From a practical standpoint I am really focusing on TV at the moment as it provides the opportunity to stay in LA. When I direct a feature like *The Howling: Reborn*, I'm away from my family for long stretches (preproduction, shooting, post) and it's too hard. And from a creative standpoint I need to feel invested.

The Howling: Reborn was personal to me because so much of what I wrote on that film was for and about my kids (who make a cameo with my wife Kristi in the final scene where the masses watch Will on the jumbotron in Times Square). For instance, the character of Will was named for my newborn son. Through that character there was so much I wanted to say to him about how I hope he will try to walk the line between strength and compassion as he grows into a man. And I often thought of my daughter Emma as I wrote Eliana... hoping she knew she was strong enough to always follow her heart and survive the consequences of doing so. So, to direct an instalment now that likely wouldn't be as personal would be hard for me.

If I did, I would do so much differently. But mostly I would insist on a budget, schedule and vision for the film that I, as a movie-goer... as a werewolf fan.... as a former studio exec... believe would produce something fresh and exciting that would bring in old fans and new. If not, what's the point? Why not just watch the original *Howling* or *American Werewolf In London* again?

ON WHETHER *THE HOWLING: REBORN*'S SLOW BUILD WILL STAND UP TO THE NEXT GENERATION OF CINEMA-GOERS:

Part of that "slow build" was intentional so that you hopefully grew invested in Will and Eliana enough to care what happened once the shit hits the fan. But that said, there were two very cool werewolf scenes that were cut from the first act of the film alone (just two of the many casualties of last minute cuts and late costume deliveries). So, if we had shot the film as intended there may have been enough action up top that we wouldn't be pondering the question.

In a macro sense, with today's streaming and

ADD media culture, I worry that the slow burn is becoming a casualty... but more so for those who don't see a film on the big screen. I think, even today, that when you buy a ticket and sit in a theater you are a little more patient with a story. For instance, when I saw *The Howling: Reborn* in a theater with an audience they always laughed at the right places and seemed interested and invested until the monsters finally appeared.

But ultimately, I think even the initial distance we've had from the release of the film has only helped the film's reception. So, I have faith the trend will continue. Based on the reactions I get from execs, folks who reach out on social media, high school and college kids I meet, etc. I have hope that *The Howling: Reborn* will continue to be discovered and still hold up for the next generation of moviegoers. ∎

8.

The Ivana Milicevic interview

Howling VII: New Moon Rising's stigma had finally flown the franchise nest and the *The Howling* was finally looking ready to be presented to an all-new generation of movie-goer.

New Moon Rising was by no means a success and it had officially brought closure to one of the most financially successful werewolf franchises in history, but producers were willing to roll the dice one more time and come full circle with an inventive post-modern wink to the franchise lycanthropic craze.

The eighth instalment in the series was originally planned as a theatrical release and to be presented in 3D. It was a modern crossover that blurred the lines between creature feature and high school morality tale with edgy *Dawson Creek* dialogue.

With *The Howling: Reborn* complete the film was released just as the werewolf and vampire popularity was undeniably on the downswing and the horror landscape had begun to change once more.

While *The Howling: Reborn* found a way to live up to its earlier practical effect past while carving out a few new terrors in new ways a glut of werewolf movies had been released in the twenty-tens, in no small measure due to the success of *Twilight*, which had established itself as the world's reigning champion in modern teen terror. *Reborn* didn't stand a chance!

Casino Royale's Ivana Milicevic, who plays *The Howling: Reborn*'s central villain, feels much differently about the film, and here's what she had to say about her wolf project.

IVANA MILICEVIC

WORKING ON A LOW-BUDGET REBOOT:
It was a really difficult film to get made. Here we are with a bunch of actors, kids mainly, and you don't have a lot of money or time to do it in. That shooting schedule was three and a half weeks. You do the best that you can to try to give it nuances. Had we have had three or four months to do that movie, it would be even better because the actors involved were really good, and you have all these constraints and things that happen, like when Landon got a really bad eye infection because of the contacts one day. It's normal stuff that happens, and on a regular movie you would have time to recoup.

In some scenes we could only shoot from one side, and that makes it difficult for a performer to find their way, but everybody was trying their best to do something good. We're all actors, and we obviously all wish we had tons of time and really explore the characters. It's one thing when it's on the page; it's another thing when we get there on the set. No-one sets out to do something mediocre ever. When we were done shooting, I was like, "Now I'm ready to shoot this movie!" We all felt like that.

ON *THE HOWLING* FRANCHISE:
All I ever saw was the original, which is so, so good, especially for what it did at the time. It's really difficult to make interesting movies, especially about werewolves, especially today.

ON TAKING THE ROLE:

What I liked about the part in particular was that I got to play all these different aspects. I got to play this motherly, seductress, maternal character. I kind of liked that there was both of these things, which are powerful. Then in the beginning, she was normal. But that kind of got cut out, so all you saw were these little bits and pieces.

I also liked the aspect how she wants her baby back. She wasn't in his life for a long time because she was forming her army. In that time, she learned that Will's powers weren't going to come to be until then, so that's why she came back for him.

All that was really fun for me, and usually I'm pretty scared of horror movies. I don't watch them because they scare me.

ON PREPARING FOR THE REBOOT:
I saw a bunch of werewolf movies when I was trying to prepare for it. It's a reboot for today, given what people are interested in. But like I said, I'm not a horror buff.

ON TRANSITIONING FROM COMEDY PRINCESS TO QUEEN OF THE WOLF PACK:
So far, so good! I used to be the comedy girl and there are times these days where I miss comedy. I bruise easy but I like the physicality of what I'm doing. I enjoy being a badass and Kathryn has many emotional depths and it all goes hand in hand. It's so out there and so bonkers and I loved it. I want to touch every pocket of the world so it's good.

ON THE FILM'S OEDIPAL IDEAS:
I kind of wanted to do it that way. It puts kind of a creepy side to it. There are a lot of issues in relationships where the boy does need to pick his girlfriend over his mother or his wife over his mother at some point. I'm not saying it's sexual. It's just life. I liked the idea of being creepy like that, but I hope it's not too much.

ON JOE NIMZIKI AS A DIRECTOR:
He was great to work with, because he used to work with the studios. They would go to the screenings, this is what always happens with movies, they go to the screenings, and the audience says, "Oh, I wish it had this kind of ending". They fix the movie according to that. He always had that hat on his head and he was always trying to make it better as we were going along. He was trying to foresee what an audience would want, what they wouldn't like. So it was interesting to have someone with that perspective on the day. He would come in and fix things on the day of shooting, when other people would wait until the film was almost finished.

ON WORKING WITH LANDON LIBOIRON & CO:
I loved working with all of those kids. They called me Mama all the time, it's kind of funny. We all really had a good time together. Landon's a really good actor. We would all get together. We would try to make the movie as good as it can be, because it's still a low-budget, and we didn't have too much time for shooting. There weren't a lot of takes, and we were just trying to make the best thing we could make, under the circumstances. We had to shoot really creatively and really fast! ∎

Image Credits

Every effort has been made to source and contact copyright holders. If any omissions do occur, the publisher will be happy to give full credit in subsequent reprints and editions.

{t} = top {b} = bottom

Cat People © 1982 RKO Pictures, Universal Pictures 12{t}, 14{t}
The Howling book © 1986 Fawcett 13{b}, 14{t}
Gary Brandner © 2018 Above The Line Agency, Rimagreer 11, 13{b}, 43{b}
Return of The Howling © 1982 Fawcett 13(b), 73{b}
The Howling: First Blood artwork © 2018 Matt Erin 16, 17, 18, 19, 20
Motel Hell © 1980 Camp Hill 23{t}
Alligator © 1980 Alligator Inc. 23{b}
Piranha © 1978 Piranha Productions, New World Pictures 24{t}
Jaws 3 People 0 © 1983 Universal Pictures, Alan Landsburg Productions 24{b}
Cat People book © 1982 Fawcett 12{b}, 14{t}
The Brain Eaters © 1985 Fawcett 39{t}
The Howling © 1981 Herald Film Company, David Allen, Peter Kuran 16, 22{t}, 32
Dee Wallace © 2018 iamdeewallace.com 34
Howling II vinyl © 1985 Filmtrax 39{b}
Philippe Mora © 2018 Philippe Mora 6, 7, 44, 50-54{t}, 55, 56, back cover
Howling III: The Marsupials © 1987 Vista Home Video, Philippe Mora 54{b}
Howling IV © 1988 IVE, Screen Media Ventures llc, Prism Leisure Corp. 62, 74{b}, back cover
Howling IV soundtrack © 1988 Justin Hayward, Lauren Danielle, Antonio Vivaldi, Barry Guard 71{b}
Bill Forsche © 2018 www.forschedesigns.com 8, 14{t}, 62-69, 71{t}, 74{t}, 77, 83{b}, 84{t}, 84{b}, 85, 87{t}, 88, 89, 96{t}, back cover
Susanne Severeid © 2018 Severeid Communications. Photo copyright Tony Van courtesy Susanne Severeid, Desmond Widser 71{t}, 73{t} 78, 79{t}, 80, 81
Adam Behr © 2018 Adam Behr (Facebook) 82
Nick Benson © 2018 Nick Benson (Facebook) 84{t}, 86, 87{b}, 89
Neil Sundstrom © 2018 Neil Sundstrom 91{b}, 94, 96{b}, 97
Elizabeth Shé © 2018 Elizabeth Shé (Facebook) 92
Howling V © 1992 IVE, Timeless Media, 2000 Mainostelevisio (MTV3) 90{t}, 90{b}, 91{t}, 93{t}, 93{b}, 95{t}, 99{t}, 99{b}, 113{b}, 115{t}, back cover
Mark Sivertsen © 2003 Mark Sivertsen 95{b}, 97, 98, 99{b}
Arledge Armenaki © 2018 Arledge Armenaki (Ace Armenaki; Tybee Dolemite) 97, 99{t}
Howling VI © 1990 Guild Home Video, 1991 August Entertainment, Trina Jones, Richard Reams, 1993 Concorde Video, 2001 Prism Leisure Corp., 2003 Artisan Entertainment, 2004 Astro Distribution (DE), 2006 Timeless Media, 2018 Feast Management 100{t}, 101{b}, 103{t}, 105{t}, 105{b}, 106{t}, 106{b}, 107, back cover
Richard Reams © 2018 Richard Reams 100{b}, 101{t}, 103{b}, 106{t}, 106{b}, 107, 108, 109{t}, 109{b}, 110{b}, 111{b}, back cover
Edward J Pei © 2018 Edward J Pei 100{b}, 101{t}, 105{t}, 106{t}, 106{b}, 107, 109{t}
Hope Perello © 2018 Hope Perello 102, 104, 106{t}, 107, 109{t}, 110{b}, 115{t}
Howling VII © Live Entertainment, New Line Cinema 112{t}, 113{t}
Leprechaun 3 © 1995 Blue Rider Pictures 113{b}
Candyman 2: Farewell to Flesh © 1995 Polygram Filmed Entertainment, Propaganda Films 113{b}
Texas Chainsaw Massacre: The Next Generation © 1994 Genre Pictures, Return Productions, Ultra Muchos Productions 113{b}
Warlock 2: The Armageddon © 1993 Trimark Pictures, Tapestry Films 114
Sorority Babes: In the Slimeball Bowl-o-Rama aka **The Imp** aka **Imp** © 1988 Empire Pictures, Beyond Infinity, Titan Productions, Jizz Films 116
Creepzoids © 1987 Titan Productions 116
Project: Metalbeast © 1995 Blue Ridge Entertainment 117{b}
The Dentist 2 © 1998 Trimark Pictures, Pierre David, Image Organization 117{b}
Return to Horror High © 1987 New World Pictures, Balcor Film Investors, Anchor Bay Entertainment 117{t}
Adventures in Dinosaur City © 1991 Smart Egg Pictures, kerkira@aquariustv.gr 117{t}
The Howling: Reborn © 2011 Moonstone Entertainment, Joe Nimziki, Benoit Beaulieu 5{b}, 118{t}, 119{t}, 121{t}, 121{b}, 122{b}, 123, 124, 125, 126{t}, 126{b}, 127{t}, 127{b}, 128, 129, 130, 131, 133, 134{t}, 135
© Associated Press 54{b}, 93{b}
The Howling © 1981 Embassy Pictures front cover, 5{t}, 13{b}, 15, 16, 21, 22{b}, 23{t}, 25-29, 31, 33, 35-37, back cover
Howling II: Your Sister is a Werewolf © 1985 Hemdale, Philippe Mora, Geoffrey Stephenson, Prop Store 7, 13{b}, 38, 39{t}, 40-42, 43{t}, 43{b}, 45-47, 49, back cover
Howling III: The Marsupials © 1987 Bancannia Holdings Pty. Ltd., Philippe Mora, Lewis Irving 50-54{t}, 55, 57, 59-61
Howling IV: The Original Nightmare © 1988 Allied Entertainments Group PLC 62, 70, 71{t}, 72, 73{t}, 73{b}, 74{t}, 75, 76, 79{b}, 80, 81, 83{t}, 84{t}, back cover
Howling V: The Rebirth © 1989 Allied Vision front cover, 91{b}, 93{t}, 95{b}, 97, 99{t}, 99{b}, 113{b}, back cover
Howling VI: The Freaks © 1991 Allied Entertainments Group PLC 100{t}, 101{b}, 102, 103{t}, 105{b}, 106{t}, 106{b}, 110{b}, 111{t}, back cover
Howling VII: New Moon Rising © 1995 Allied Entertainments Group PLC 112{b}, 113{t}, 114
The Howling: Reborn © 2011 Anchor Bay Films 118{b}, 119{b}, 120, 121{t}, 122{t}, 126{t}, 126{b}, 127{t}, 127{b}, 130, 131, 132, 134{b}, 135, back cover